T0105512

# THE CROSS TRAP

## A LAYMAN'S THEORY

## ELMER M. HAYGOOD

iUNIVERSE, INC.
NEW YORK   BLOOMINGTON

# The Cross Trap
## A Layman's Theory

iUniverse books may be ordered through booksellers or by contacting:

iUniverse
1663 Liberty Drive
Bloomington, IN 47403
www.iuniverse.com
1-800-Authors (1-800-288-4677)

Because of the dynamic nature of the Internet, any Web addresses or
links contained in this book may have changed since publication and may
no longer be valid.

ISBN: 978-1-4401-7625-8 (sc)
ISBN: 978-1-4401-7626-5 (ebk)

Library of Congress Control Number: 2009910942

Printed in the United States of America

iUniverse rev. date: 12/30/2014

# CONTENTS

# INTRODUCTION

I have written this book to encourage in-depth scriptural study on the part of the average Christian, the layman. Each layman, regardless of his position in a Christian organization, should seek to learn more about the scriptures through his personal research and personal communion with God. It is understood that such research is not required for personal salvation; however, this continuous association with biblical passages should instill in each individual a hunger for deeper understanding. For the layman to engage in a quest for understanding, as would be expected of those in leadership, is of great benefit to any Christian organization; such increased knowledge elevates the entire group. As he continues his studies, certain areas of information will evoke a greater curiosity and lead to even more in-depth study.

One area of biblical study that certainly stands out among the rest is the Crucifixion of Jesus Christ. This lies at the heart of our Christian faith; thus it is important to fully recognize the totality of the spiritual and physical struggles Jesus endured on the cross. With this book, I intend to encourage a closer look into the real background for the events at the cross. The cross was more than an instrument for death. It was, more importantly to the religious leaders, a well-conceived and almost perfect trap that was set to destroy Jesus' body and his name in history. The religious leaders devised a plan that would make it a violation of the Law for anyone to teach of Jesus, the accused blasphemer, false teacher, and sorcerer. If they could prove that Jesus was teaching a false doctrine, then whoever perpetuated that doctrine would be guilty of the same act against the Law. The religious authorities wanted the Crucifixion to be the last act of Jesus' life and the final mention of him in Jewish history. They were challenged with how to destroy such a popular figure through legal means. They were preparing for a post-Crucifixion spin that would portray Jesus as a false prophet who could not possibly be the Son of God. I refer to the plan they devised as the "cross trap."

Were thirty pieces of silver really given to Judas simply to identify Jesus? Judas indeed gave them Jesus through his kiss, but he also gave them the key element for the trap: he provided information on Jesus' commitment to an ancient rite of consecration called the Vow of the Nazirite, as recorded in the Book of Numbers. This information was vital to the religious leaders' attempt to accuse Jesus of violating the Laws of Moses and to prove that he was not the Messiah and definitely not the Son of God.

This book takes a closer look at all the commonly highlighted items, people, and activities surrounding the Crucifixion. The Crucifixion scene is always depicted with three crosses. The execution of the two thieves was not prescheduled; it was part of the trap being set for Jesus. The two thieves were handpicked by the religious leaders to die with him and were probably very feeble men. The vinegar and gall provided at the cross were not selected arbitrarily. The gambling among the soldiers and the railing by the people at the foot of the cross were all part of the choreographed events the religious leaders had planned. Jesus' call to the Father while on the cross was one of desperation. He recognized the trap in which he had been placed and asked God whether he was going to allow the trap to fulfill its purpose. The soldier piercing Jesus' body with a spear was God's response to the trap and the answer to Jesus' desperate cry.

The purposes of this book are twofold: to show how all elements of the final hours of Jesus' trial and crucifixion were intertwined as one plot and to describe the raging spiritual battle occurring at the cross that went to the final moment of Jesus' life. All of the events surrounding the Crucifixion were an attack on Jesus' status as a priest and as one who could make judgments on righteousness and the forgiveness of sins. Even though this book mentions the conflicts between Jesus and the religious authorities, in the end it will show that the true influence of the cross trap is Satan, who is the noted antagonist of Jesus Christ.

The scriptures used in this book are from the *Scofield Study Bible,* 1976 edition, authorized King James version, Oxford Press, Inc.

# CHAPTER 1:
# THE FOUNDATION FOR THE
# CROSS TRAP

The foundation for the cross trap set by the religious leaders was based on Jesus' commitment to an ancient rite of consecration called the Vow of the Nazirite, which had maintained its strong religious significance during the time of his ministry. This vow was a voluntary consecration to God for a specific period of time and contained strict guidelines such as abstinence and the proper way to begin and end the vow. These are outlined in Numbers 6:1–21. The first eleven verses will be the primary focus of this book:

> Numbers 6:1-9 -And the Lord spoke unto Moses, saying, Speak unto the children of Israel, and say unto them, When either man or woman shall separate themselves to vow a Vow of the Nazirite, to separate themselves unto the Lord, He shall separate himself from wine and strong drink, and shall drink no vinegar of wine, or vinegar of strong drink,

neither shall he drink any liquor of grapes, nor eat moist grapes, or dried. All the days of his separation shall he eat nothing that is made of the vine tree, from the kernel even to the husk. All the days of the vow of his separation there shall no razor come upon his head; until the days are fulfilled, in the which he separateth himself unto the Lord, he shall be holy, and shall let the locks of his head grow. All the days that he separateth himself unto the Lord, he shall come at no dead body. He shall not make himself unclean for his father, or for his mother, for his brother, or for his sister, when they die, because the consecration of his God is upon his head. All the days of his consecration he is holy unto the Lord. And if any man die very suddenly by him, and he hath defiled the head of his consecration, then he shall shave his head in the day of his cleansing, on the seventh day shall he shave it.

Defilement of the individual through violations of the conditions of the vow was considered a sin that required a sin offering with the assistance of the priest.

Numbers 6:11 And the priest shall offer the one for a sin offering, and make atonement for him, because he sinned by the dead, and shall hallow his head the same day.

Prior to the Crucifixion, Jesus entered into the Vow of the Nazirite: he showed the outward signs of his consecration and made an audible statement of commitment during the Last Supper and the commencement of Communion. During the Last Supper and the institution of Communion, Jesus told the disciples he would not drink of the fruit of the vine until he went to the Father. This statement directly correlates with the Vow of the Nazirite. (Also, Jesus had begun to allow his hair to grow.)

> Matthew 26:29 But I say unto you, I will not drink henceforth of the fruit of the vine, until that day when I drink it new with you in my Father's kingdom.

> Mark 14:25 Verily I say unto you, I will drink no more of the fruit of the vine, until that day that I drink it new in the kingdom of God.

> Luke 22:18 For I say unto you, I will not drink of the fruit of the vine, until the kingdom of God shall come.

The Vow of the Nazirite required strong personal discipline in refraining from its forbidden acts. A man who is nailed to the cross is extremely vulnerable to any circumstances that arise that may be contrary to the dictates of the vow. Judas was given a handsome reward of thirty pieces of silver because he reported to the high priest that he had heard Jesus pronounce his commitment to the Vow of the Nazirite. The chief priests and other religious leaders expected this vow to give them specific legal rights to discredit Jesus under Mosaic Law while they used his death to save the nation, as the chief priest had suggested in John 11:50. The religious leaders were the keepers and the enforcers of the Law; thus they acted as accuser, judge, and jury for violations.

The significance of the Vow of the Nazirite is indicated by the dedication of a complete chapter in the Book of Numbers and other references to it in the Bible and in biblical histories.

> Amos 2:11 -And I raised up of your sons for prophets, and of your young men for Nazirites, Is it not even thus O ye children of Israel? Saith the Lord.

The practice of taking on the Vow of the Nazirite was and continues to be an integral part of Jewish Law.

> Halakha (Jewish Law) has a rich tradition on the laws of the Nazirite ... From the perspective of Orthodox Judaism, these laws are not a historical curiosity but can be practiced even today. However, since there is no temple in Jerusalem to complete the vow, and any vow would be permanent, modern rabbinical authorities strongly discourage the practice to the point where it is almost unheard of today. (Wikipedia: www. wikipedia.org/Nazirite)

These temporary Nazarites seem to have been
very numerous. They are mentioned in the
Maccabean period (I Macc. iii. 49), in the
time of Herod Agrippa I. (Josephus, "Ant."
xix. 6, § 1; *idem*, "B. J." ii. 15, § 1), and
later in the mishnaic tractate Nazir. (Jewish
Encyclopedia
http://www.jewishencyclopedia.com/view.
jsp?letter=N&artid=142)

The Vow of the Nazirite had two primary restrictions:
the avoidance of any drink made from the fruit of the
vine and the avoidance of the dead. In view of these
two restrictions, the religious leaders concluded that
this particular area of Mosaic Law conformed to their
desire to see Jesus crucified by the Roman government.
The Jewish method of capital punishment was stoning;
however, the Jewish nation was under the rule of the
Roman government, and at the time of Jesus' ministry,
capital punishment was performed by crucifixion.

Crucifixion was in use particularly among
the Persians, Seleucids, Carthaginians, and
Romans from about the 6th century BC to
the 4th century AD, when in the year 337
Emperor Constantine I abolished it in his
empire, out of veneration for Jesus Christ,
the most famous victim of crucifixion. It has
sometimes been used even in modern times.
(http://en.wikipedia.org/wiki/Crucifixion)

The religious leaders needed to convince Pilate, the Roman governor, that Jesus had violated a Roman law worthy of punishment by crucifixion. At the same time, they wanted to use a Jewish law to discredit his name and priestly status. Since Jesus had convinced people he was the Messiah, the returning Davidic king, and the Son of God, there was the chance of convincing Pilate that Jesus was guilty of sedition against the Roman government.

> Sedition is a term of <u>law</u> which refers to covert conduct, such as <u>speech</u> and <u>organization</u>, that is deemed by the legal authority as tending toward <u>insurrection</u> against the established order. Sedition often includes <u>subversion</u> of a <u>constitution</u> and <u>incitement</u> of discontent (or <u>resistance</u>) to lawful authority. Sedition may include any commotion, though not aimed at direct and open violence against the laws. ( http://en.wikipedia.org/wiki/Crucifixion)

The religious leaders had to find a violation of a Roman law whose penalty was capital punishment because Rome would not allow a sentence of death for violating a Jewish law. If they were successful, they could put Jesus on the cross, helpless to avoid the presence of the dead and struggling to avoid the consumption of a forbidden drink.

> For Jewish leaders of the time, there were serious concerns about Roman rule and an insurgent <u>Zealot</u> movement in <u>Beit Shammai</u> to eject the Romans from <u>Israel</u>. The Romans

would not perform execution over violations of <u>Jewish law</u>, and therefore the charge of blasphemy would not have mattered to Pilate. Caiaphas' legal position, therefore, was to establish that Jesus was guilty not only of blasphemy, but also of proclaiming himself the <u>messiah</u>, which was understood as the return of the <u>Davidic</u> king. This would have been an act of sedition and prompted Roman execution.
(h t t p : / / e n . w i k i p e d i a . o r g / w i k i / Caiaphas#Matthew:_trial_of_Jesus)

The religious leaders always attacked Jesus on the issues covered by Mosaic Law because that was what separated true teaching from false. However, when they questioned him, they found it extremely difficult to trap him because he indeed knew and abided within the letter and spirit of the Law.

> Matthew 22:15–18 - Then went the Pharisees, and took counsel how they might entangle him in his talk. And they sent out unto him their disciples with the Herodians, saying, Master, we know that thou art true, and teachest the way of God in truth, neither carest thou for any man; for thou regardest not the person of men. Tell us, therefore, What thinkest thou? Is it lawful to give tribute unto Caesar, or not? But Jesus perceived their wickedness, and said, Why test me, ye hypocrite?

> Luke 11:53–54 - And as he said these things unto them, the scribes and the Pharisees began to oppose him vehemently, and to provoke him to speak of many things, Laying wait for him, and seeking to catch something out of his mouth that they might accuse him.

It seems strange that the religious sects and priests would attack Jesus if he was teaching the laws of God truthfully. They questioned him, and in all the instances he answered them in an appropriate manner without having spoken a word of untruth. The attacks on Jesus indeed seemed to be acts of envy, for Jesus acted in a priest's capacity but had not joined the ranks to become one of them. As far as the religious leaders were concerned, Jesus was a carpenter's son who felt called to the service of the people and who took on priestly status through the Vow of the Nazirite as others had done. But Jesus' miracles and the crowds that sought him revealed that he was an exceptional teacher, prophet, and priest. He soon became a thorn to the envious chief priests and elders.

Therefore, the religious leaders needed a plan that would put Jesus on the cross and that would bring shame upon him, showing him to be a false teacher, blasphemer, and sorcerer—definitely not the Son of God. Judas' report gave them hope that there was finally an area of Mosaic Law that could sustain an accusation against Jesus. This particular area of the law, which outlined a voluntary consecration to God and the establishment of a priestly nature, was ideal for the cross trap because it required no questioning of Jesus and the religious authorities would be in complete control of the setting and the potential outcomes.

The key expectations of the cross trap with regard to the Vow of the Nazirite are these: 1) Jesus would be tempted to drink the fruit of the vine; 2) he would be placed on the cross in the presence of two dying men and eventually be in the presence of the dead; 3) he would be unable to cleanse himself of the violation of being associated with the dead; 4) he would receive no assistance from the priesthood for the required cleansing; and 5) he would be tempted to miraculously come down off the cross and flee from the dying thieves in order to keep his vow to his Father. The Law gave explicit instructions concerning vows, as can be found in the book of Deuteronomy:

> Deuteronomy 23:21–23 When thou shalt vow a vow unto the Lord thy God, thou shalt not be slack to pay; for the Lord thy God will surely require it of thee, and it would be sin unto thee. But if thou shalt forbear to vow, it shall be no sin in thee. That which is gone out of thy lips thou shalt keep and perform, even a freewill offering, according as thou hast vowed unto the Lord thy God, which thou hast promised with thy mouth.

A few exceptional circumstances have been recorded in which a Nazirite was allowed to start his period of consecration over again after a violation, but a man who is nailed to the cross and is expected to die would not have the opportunity for such an exception. Any violation that occurred while on the cross would be permanent and without atonement.

With Jesus having voluntarily entered into this period of consecration, the religious authorities planned to use this law of consecration to send the Son of God back to God as a sinner. This would be accomplished by forcing him to be involved in a forbidden act and making it impossible for him to be able to perform the required acts for cleansing or forgiveness of his sin. The religious leaders did not believe in Jesus as the Messiah or the Lamb of God whose purpose was to take away the sins of the world; however, their plot, if successful, would have made him an unworthy sacrifice for man's sins.

> Lamb of God is one of the titles given to Jesus in the New Testament and consequently in the Christian tradition. It refers to Jesus' role as a sacrifice atoning for the sins of man in Christian theology, harkening back to ancient Hebrew sacrifices in which a lamb was slain during the passover. In the original Passover in Egypt, the blood was smeared on the door posts and lintel of each household (Exodus 12:1-28).
> (Wikipedia.org,http://en.wikipedia.org/wiki/Lamb_of_God)

# Chapter 2:
# The Nazirite Star

The Vow of the Nazirite was a well-known rite of consecration that made priests of common men. It had notable restrictions but probably also had many benefits and responsibilities. The responsibilities may have varied from those of the regular priests. The priests of Aaron and the Levites were appointed by God for the maintenance and activities of the tabernacle and later, the temple. However, there were probably many spiritual issues to be dealt with in the population that could not be handled immediately by the priests at the temple.

> Simply put, rabbis are not priests, but rather regular Jews who have chosen to take on this extra religious obligation to serve their fellow Jews in the capacities of ministers, teachers, counselors, etc. People who enter the rabbinate have done so to dedicate themselves to God in a way that goes above and beyond the regular religious obligations of being a Jewish adult and as such are similar to the Nazirite described in Naso.

(D'Varim, http://dvarim11.blogspot.com/2008/06/from-nazirite-to-modern-rabbi)

In the order of the Nazirite there is not only the concept of separation and consecration of an individual to God but also the concept of ministerial service, and perhaps a link to the royal priesthood as found in the High Priest's vow of service.
(Agape Bible Study, Vow of the Nazirite, www.agapebiblestudy.com

The consecration of the Nazirite in some ways resembled that of the priests, and similar words are used of both in <u>Lev 21:12</u> and <u>Nu 6:17</u>, the priest's vow being even designated nezer. It opened up the way for any Israelite to do special service on something like semi-sacerdotal lines.
(http://net.bible.org/dictionary.php?word=NAZIRITE)

In the desert Moses divided the Israelites among captains, but they were not necessarily spiritual leaders. God allowed for the unction or the "calling" in specially consecrated individuals who could minister to the people; this ministry was sanctioned by the Vow of the Nazirite. The practice continued from ancient times to Jesus' lifetime and was incorporated into part of Paul's ministry. Some of Jesus' activities and actions seem to imply that, even though he was the Son of God, he also engaged in the consecration of the Vow of the Nazirite. There is the possibility that he took the vow on more than one occasion, as did Paul, the apostle. What is recorded at the Last Supper as a statement pertaining to the Vow of the Nazirite probably concerned his current vow.

> Matthew 26:29 But I say unto you, I will not drink henceforth of the fruit of the vine, until that day when I drink it new with you in my Father's kingdom.

> "As to the duration of a Nazarite's vow, everyone was left at liberty to fix his own time. There is mention made in Scripture of only three who were Nazarites for life: Samson, Samuel, and John the Baptist (Judges 13:4, 5; I Samuel 1:11; Luke 1:15). In its ordinary form, however, the Nazarite's vow lasted only thirty and, at the most, one hundred days. (NetBible, www. Netbible.org/dictionary/Nazarite)

> While the usual time was thirty days, two or more additional vows were generally taken, in which case each period was regarded as a separate Nazariteship, to be immediately followed, when duly completed, by the succeeding one (Maimonides, "Yad," Nezirut, iii. 6). (Jewish Encyclopedia, http://www. jewishencyclopedia.com, nazirite)

The Bible mentions that Jesus went to the temple on a daily basis and began to teach. Is it conceivable that the same religious authorities who wanted to get a hold of Jesus in the crowds would allow him to simply sit in their temple and teach? There had to be a controlling matter covered by the Jewish law that allowed Jesus to enter the temple and teach. There had to be more than his popularity status as a prophet or great teacher. When Jesus asked for the books, he received from temple storage the same books that the scribes and the high priest had received for their teachings. It is also astonishing that Jesus would be allowed to teach in the temple when some among the religious leaders considered him to be a false teacher, a blasphemer, and even a sorcerer. It would seem that the temple would be the most unlikely place for Jesus' teachings. Still, he taught there daily even after he had overturned the tables of the vendors.

> Luke 19:45 And he went into the temple, and began to cast out them that sold, and them that bought.

> Luke 19:47–48 And he taught daily in the temple. But the chief priest, and the scribes, and the chief of the people, sought to destroy him. But could not find what they might do, for all the people were very attentive to hear him.

If Luke 19:45 and 47 are a correct progression of activities, it is amazing that Jesus overturned the tables in the temple and was not attacked for his actions by anyone present. Why? Was it because he was Jesus Christ? It is common knowledge that merchants, especially traveling merchants, are very conscious of being robbed. This fear was understandably greater during the Passover when there was the opportunity for much profit. Thus it is highly probable that many of the merchants were armed with daggers. Yet none of them dared to take a hold of Jesus or threaten him with bodily harm. The high priest, who stood to benefit the most from the festivities of the Passover, would have arranged for crowd control and security in the temple. Why, then, was Jesus untouched after his aggressive actions? Is it possible that at the time he was recognized as a Nazirite priest and therefore not to be touched by the common people? Jesus, the Nazirite priest, would have been considered the responsibility of the priesthood, and all complaints would have been forwarded to the priesthood for action. It was also the high priest who was apt to lose the most from a disruption in the temple.

> In ancient times the priests were persons dedicated to God (Ezek. xliv. 20; I Sam. i. 11), and it follows from the juxtaposition of prophets and Nazarites (Amos ii. 11–12) that the latter must have been regarded as in a sense priests.
> (Jewish Encyclopedia.com, Nazarite Laws)

> The high priest was the head of all priests.
> (Jewish Encyclopedia.com, High Priest)

> The high priest and his family were among the richest people of the land in the time of Christ, making enormous profits out of the sacrifices and temple business.
> (NetBible, http://net.bible.org/dictionary. php?word=Priest, %20High)

The Nazirite, the person entering into the vow, had a status equal to or perhaps greater than that of the high priest. The requirements of abstinence and cleansing were in some areas about the same for the Nazirite priest and the high priest, and in other areas even more stringent than for the high priest.

> "Many have observed that these restrictions are similar to those of the kohanim (priests), but, in fact, the Nazirite's restrictions were even greater than the priest's. ... So, it appears that, for the period of the vow, the Nazarite's sanctity surpassed even that of the High Priest." (conservapedia.com/nazirite)

Then there is the account of the woman caught in adultery, which truly raises questions as to the legal status of Jesus' ministry. The story is a very familiar one, but why does it exist at all?

> John 8:35 And the scribes and Pharisees brought unto him a woman taken in adultery; and when they had set her in the midst. They say unto him, Master, this woman was taken in adultery, in the very act. Now Moses, in

the law, commanded us that such should be
stoned; but what sayest thou?

One of the key elements of the story is that the scribes and
the Pharisees initiated the event. Why did the keepers of
the Law bring someone to Jesus for an interpretation of
the Law and a decision on sin? Was it simply because Jesus
was a well-beloved teacher of the scriptures? This was not
a case to be solved by a parable; rather, this was an urgent
case of a real-life incident. The decision would be an
immediate, life-changing one. It's simply not conceivable
that just having the status of an anointed teacher would
also imply the right to make such judgments. The scribes
and Pharisees definitely did not accept Jesus's status
as the Son of God, and the common people did not
understand that status. They better understood the role
of the Nazirite priest. Jesus' judgment was accepted as
final and was acted upon without hesitation. The scribes'
and Pharisees' actions implied that indeed Jesus had the
legal authority to make such decisions. He exercised
the same authority to convict or absolve as the regular
religious authorities at the time.

Bible discussions of Jesus' ministry cover many cities,
but it must be understood that in each city Jesus had to
operate within the laws of that region. He was not given
the keys to the cities in order to enter the synagogues
and to have impromptu gatherings. Each city, though
Jewish, was under the rule of the Roman Empire and
its appointed authorities. The period of Jesus' ministry
was also a time of increasing tension between the Jews
and the Romans because of the Jewish insurgency. The
high priest, who oversaw all religious activities, was

concerned about the influence of insurgents and zealots, and the movements of Jesus and his disciples were closely monitored.

> By 63 BCE, the partially <u>Hellenized</u> territory had come under <u>Roman</u> imperial rule as a valued crossroads to trading territories. The Roman <u>Prefect</u>'s first duty to Rome was to maintain order, through his political appointee the <u>High Priest</u>. In general, notably from 7 to 26 CE, <u>Roman Judea</u> was peaceful and self-managed, although <u>riots</u>, sporadic rebellions, and <u>violent resistance</u> were an ongoing risk. The conflict between the Jews' demand for religious independence and Rome's efforts to impose a common system of governance upon its entire empire (including in religious and cultural matters, see also <u>Romanization (cultural)</u>) meant there was a constant underlying tension alongside peaceful governance, with minor outbreaks common.
> http://en.wikipedia.org/wiki/Jesus_in_a_cultural_and_historical_background

The freedom of movement and the authority to judge were probably granted to him by the priestly status incorporated in the Vow of the Nazirite. Possibly the best example of the application of the Vow of the Nazirite in ministry was shown by the apostle Paul.

Acts 21:24, 26 (24) Them take, and purify thyself with them, and pay their expenses, that they may shave their heads, and all may know that those things, of which they were informed concerning thee, are nothing, but that thou thyself also walkest orderly, and keepest the law. (26) Then Paul took the men, and the next day, purifying himself with them, entered into the temple to signify the accomplishment of the days of purification, until an offering should be offered for every one of them.

Acts 18:18 And Paul after this tarried there yet a good while, and then took his leave of the brethren, and sailed from there into Syria, and with him Priscilla and Aquila; Paul having shorn his head in Cenchrea; for he had a vow.

In the Book of Acts Paul entered into the Vow of the Nazirite on more than one occasion and there have been some questions as to why he assumed that role. Perhaps it allowed his legal entry, without question, into certain regions, and it may have been a familiar point of confidence for some people in responding to his ministry. Jesus went to many areas, some remote, as the Nazirite priest with the power to heal, perform miracles, and forgive sin, and Paul went to some of the same areas as a Nazirite priest to explain Jesus the priest and the Son of God.

Jesus elevated the role of the Nazirite priest to a much higher level than was customary and than was expected by the priesthood. This new Nazirite priest formed a band of men who operated under his authority in the cities he visited and reported back to him rather than to the high priest. In the midst of the priesthood's concern about Jesus and his power to perform miracles, the priesthood discovered that his disciples had performed miracles and cast out demons: Jesus had made miracle workers of common men.

There were many Nazirite priests, but it is doubtful that any went to the temple to request the books of the Law and then begin to teach. It is also doubtful that any other Nazirite priest went to the temple to overturn the tables of the vendors. And, of course, no Nazirite priest claimed to be the Son of God. The Nazirite priests were expected to perform their service, go to the temple to announce the end of their period of consecration, cut their hair, toss their hair under the altar, and make the required offerings.

> When the period of separation was complete, the ceremonial of release had to be gone through. It consisted of the presentation of burnt, sin and peace offerings with their accompaniments as detailed in Nu 6:13–21, the shaving of the head and the burning of the hair of the head of separation, after which the Nazirite returned to ordinary life.
> (NetBible.org, http://net.bible.org/ dictionary.php?word=NAZIRITE)

When Jesus announced to the disciples that he would not drink the fruit of the vine until he drinks it new with them in his father's kingdom, he in essence said two things: 1) He could not be expected to come to the temple to announce the end of his consecration and 2) the priesthood must be prepared to tolerate him as a Nazirite priest for the rest of his life and theirs as well. The continuous ministry of Jesus meant his continued presence teaching at the temple and the continued gathering of the masses to hear him there, in the cities and even on the waters. It also meant the ongoing need to expend resources to monitor his travel and report to the Roman authorities the nature of his activities. Jesus and his band of men, as the secular world probably saw it, were a question mark in a region where much effort was being made to prevent uprisings among the Jews against the Roman rule.

Prior to the Last Supper, Jesus had raised Lazarus from the dead, which cause many to believe he was the Messiah. When he later entered Jerusalem on the path of clothes and palms that were laid out for him, it was expected that Jesus would place himself in a highly exclusive category that previously belonged to only one man named Melchizedek, the king of Salem who was also a priest. In taking the vow and riding into Jerusalem on the foal of an ass, Jesus was usurping the entire leadership of the Jewish nation. The religious leaders were viewing a man whose religious teachings were considered subversive to their own and who was in the act of fulfilling a great prophecy before their eyes. Though the crowd of people was reacting to the miracles, especially the raising of

Lazarus, the religious leaders were well aware of the implications of such an entrance into Jerusalem.

> Zechariah 9:9 Rejoice greatly, O daughter of Zion; shout, O daughter of Jerusalem; behold, thy King cometh unto thee; he is just; and having salvation; lowly, and riding upon an ass, and upon a colt, the foal of an ass.

Jesus performed this prophecy-fulfilling act during the most important religious time of the year when the high priest was supposed to be the star. But the chatter in Jerusalem was about Jesus, the number-one prospect for king. The scriptures say that the whole city of Jerusalem was moved because of Jesus' entrance.

> Matthew 21:10 And when he was come into Jerusalem, all the city was moved, saying, Who is this?

"Who is this?" must of have been in the minds of the religious leaders as they looked upon Jesus with disapproval. The people were shouting "Hosanna" as though Jesus was a king arriving in Jerusalem, but to the religious leaders he was neither a king nor a priest. Jesus did not appear to them to be the proper portrayal of the Messiah or the proper representative of the priesthood. According to Jewish history, the priest was required to be physically unblemished and rather handsome so that he could be a representative of the beauty of the temple and the perfection of God. Any blemish or imperfection was considered not beneficial to the perfect aura of the priesthood.

> Certain imperfections could disqualify a kohen (priest) from serving in the Temple. Since the Temple was a place of beauty and the services that were held in it were designed to inspire visitors to thoughts of repentance and closeness to God, a less than physically perfect kohen would mar the atmosphere. (Wikipedia.org, http://en.wikipedia.org/wiki/Kohen)

> Blemishes in Regard to Priestly Blessing: The following six blemishes disqualify a priest from pronouncing the blessing in temple or synagogue: Defective articulation of speech; malformation of face, hands or feet, or unusual appearance of hands (when, for instance, they are discolored with dye, for thus they attract the attention of the audience); moral delinquency, as idolatry or murder; insufficiency of age (his beard must be fully grown); state of inebriety; and not having washed his hands. An offspring of an unlawful marriage is debarred from the pronunciation of the blessing, because he is not considered a priest at all (Maimonides, "Nesiat Kappayim," xv.).
> (Jewish Encyclopediahttp://www.jewishencyclopedia.com, Blemishes of priests)

> Ritualistic Blemishes: The disqualifications under this head are: Levitical uncleanness; birth in unlawful wedlock, or in an unnatural way; uncertainty as to sex ( = , see Androgynos); state of mourning; or of inebriety; disheveled hair, and rent garments ("Yad," Biat ha-Mikdash).
> (Jewish Encyclopedia, http://www.jewishencyclopedia.com,blemishes)

The physical appearance of Jesus is today widely debated; however, the prophet Isaiah provided a description of the Christ and portrays a man whose appearance did not quite meet the historical priesthood's qualification for personal beauty. According to Isaiah, the physical appearance of Christ would not be appealing to the eyes but instead unattractive and not to be praised.

> Isaiah 53:2 For he shall grow up before him like a tender plant, and like a root out of a dry ground; he hath no form nor comeliness, and when we shall see him, there is no beauty that we should desire him.

Is it possible that the priesthood during Jesus' time was so focused on his failure to physically meet their qualifications that they were willing to ignore his teachings and miracles? Then there is the issue of Jesus' birth, which is historically recorded as a miraculous one. One of the disqualifying blemishes of the priesthood was an unnatural birth. But how did the priesthood consider Jesus' birth while not believing in him? By faith, Christians today accept the biblical explanation for Joseph and Mary's marriage, but we must consider the minds of those who were without faith during Jesus' time. Was Joseph and Mary's marriage questioned by the religious leaders who were antagonistic to Jesus? The fact of being an offspring of a questionable marriage was also a noted blemish in Jewish history. Did the chief priests and elders and the high priest consider Jesus a thorough contradiction to their historical requirements and a continual embarrassment to the temple in which he taught daily? Incredibly to the chief priests and elders, the same Jesus entered the holy city of Jerusalem in the role of the Messiah, the highest earthly status of the Jews, and in their opinion he did not even meet the minimum requirements for priesthood.

When Jesus entered the city on the foal of an ass, everything about him was offensive to the priesthood: the animal, the man, and the possible low priestly status afforded him by the Vow of the Nazirite. He was not on a sturdy white horse, he was not physically perfect, and he was not of the regular order of priests. Envy abounded as the throngs of people forsook the pomp of the traditional priesthood for the lowly character of Jesus Christ. Matthew 27:18 reveals that envy was one of the major factors in Jesus' crucifixion.

> Mathew 27: 17–18 Therefore, when they were gathered together, Pilate said unto them, Whom will ye that I release unto you? Barabbas, or Jesus, who is called Christ? For he knew that for envy they had delivered him.

Adding to the priesthood's increasing disdain for Jesus, Judas later reported to the high priest that in the midst of the Feast of Unleavened Bread and the Passover, Jesus had indoctrinated his disciples into a new ordinance around his own blemished body: that ordinance is today called Communion. It is highly conceivable that when Judas reported all that occurred at the Last Supper, the chief priests and elders were overwrought because Jesus was asking men to honor his body as the perfect sacrifice for sin. Yet the religious leaders considered his body to be imperfect, lacking the necessary beauty to represent the temple and God's perfection. Jesus' death became highly necessary to eliminate his teachings, his miracles, and his blemished image. There was an urgent need to prevent the spreading of his new ordinance. Also, for the continued prosperity of the Jewish nation that was trying to exist within the Roman Empire, there was a need to crush all movements, whether violent or nonviolent, to prevent Rome from viewing the area as being without proper control. In such a case Rome's eventual action would be to replace the Jewish authorities with Roman officials.

The Crucifixion, the religious leaders hoped, would refurbish the image of the priesthood and return the Sabbath as a high day with the usual commercialism and with the high priest as the star.

# CHAPTER 3:
# THE BETRAYAL

There has been much speculation on what motivated Judas to betray Jesus for thirty pieces of silver. Most of the explanations are centered on the political expectations of the Jews, the prophetic nature and spirituality of Jesus' ministry, and greed. There is also a very common occurrence in the behavior of men that could give a plausible explanation for Judas' actions. Judas had forsaken his personal ambitions for three years to follow someone he believed to be the Messiah. Most men who have sacrificed years of their lives to follow what they now believe is a failed cause find starting over to be traumatic.

And, though nothing should be allowed to palliate the guilt of the great betrayal, it may become more intelligible if we think of it as the outcome of gradual failing in lesser things. So again the repentance may be taken to imply that the traitor deceived himself by a <u>false</u> hope that after all <u>Christ</u> might pass through the midst of His enemies as He had done before at the brow of the mountain.

And though the circumstances of the death of the traitor give too much reason to fear the worst, the Sacred Text does not distinctly reject the possibility of real repentance.
(New Advent, www.newadvent.org/cathen/085391)

Matthew 26:14–16 suggests that Judas betrayed Jesus out of simple greed for the bribe money, whereas Luke 22:3 and John 13:27 say that the Devil entered into him and made him do it. But some biblical scholars have put forward another theory. They say that Judas wanted Jesus to lead a revolt against the Romans and got angry when it became clear that no revolt was planned.
(http://www.gospel-mysteries.net/judas-iscariot.html)

Perhaps, also, Judas "abandoned what seemed to him a failing cause, and hoped by his treachery to gain a position of honor and influence in the Pharisaic party."
(NetBible, www.net.bible.org/dictionary.php?word=Judas%20Iscariot

Judas was perhaps concerned about how to return to the lifestyle he had before Jesus. He knew he must do so in a land where the power of the high priest and other religious authorities loomed heavily overhead. How does he reestablish his income earning capability? How could he be employed or run a business when most of the successful employers and businessmen had been at the temple when Jesus overturned their tables during the most profitable time of the year? Some say that Judas acted out of greed, but he perhaps acted more out of what he perceived to be a great need, taking the thirty pieces of silver not just for the love of money but for the need to jumpstart a new life.

Another reason for Judas' desire to betray Jesus could have been his plans to give up his apostleship and join the Jewish insurgency. As a man who had followed a pacifist for approximately three years, he would not have been readily accepted in the resistance movement. Thus Judas may have believed that membership among the insurgents would require doing a worthy deed. Since Jesus was not encouraging a revolt against Roman rule, his ministry may have been seen as a stumbling block to the insurgents who were trying to get the ear of the masses. There was, perhaps, a belief that if Jesus could simply be arrested and held in prison for an extended length of time, the movement to resist the Roman occupation would flourish. Also, it would have been very beneficial for Judas to take an offering to the rebels, and thirty pieces of silver would have been a handsome one. He would still have to earn a rightful place among them, but they would view him in a better light. As a disciple of Jesus, Judas would have gained popularity and valuable experiences with the people, and these could have merited him a leadership role at some level, whether immediately or at some time in the near future.

There are some people that look upon Judas' kiss as an act of betrayal, but why would the act of pointing out Jesus be considered as such? Was the very public Jesus attempting to hide? Any one of the high priest's servants could have identified Jesus if he was patient enough. The religious leaders had always been able to pick him out in a crowd when they wished to take ahold of him but could not because of the crowds. Are we to believe that a kiss was the best way a man like Judas could think of to betray Jesus? Judas had plenty of time to consider what he could do that would be worthy of thirty pieces of silver.

> Matthew 26:14–16 Then one of the twelve, called Judas Iscariot, went unto the chief priests, And said unto them, What will ye give me, and I will deliver him unto you? And they bargained with him for thirty pieces of silver. And from that time he sought opportunity to betray him.

Was a kiss worth thirty pieces of silver to the high priest? The laughter in the room would have been deafening if Judas had dared to ask for money for a kiss. Judas needed to provide information to which only the disciples of Jesus were privileged. It became urgent that he pick out Jesus in the Garden of Gethsemane because he had already betrayed him by providing valuable information to the religious leaders. They were now ready to act upon that information—they were ready to set the trap. A closer look at the following scriptures reveals that the writers indicate Judas had already betrayed Jesus prior to the kiss.

> Matthew 26:48 Now, he that betrayed him gave them a sign …

Mark 14:44 And he that betrayed him had given them a sign …

John 18:5 They answered him, Jesus, of Nazareth. Jesus saith unto them, I am he. And Judas, also, who betrayed him, stood with them.

The information Judas provided the chief priest that was worthy of thirty pieces of silver was partially gleaned from Jesus' conversation with the disciples at the Last Supper. Jesus tells them of his commitment to the Vow of the Nazirite, as indicated in the following scriptures:

Matthew 26:29—But I say unto you, I will not drink henceforth of the fruit of the vine, until that day when I drink it new with you in my Father's kingdom.

Mark 14:25—Verily I say unto you, I will drink no more of the fruit of the vine, until that day that I drink it new in the kingdom of God.

Luke 22:18—For I say unto you, I will not drink of the fruit of the vine, until the kingdom of God shall come.

Judas was at the table when Jesus said he had refrained from drinking the fruit of the vine. He was able to personally witness that Jesus had entered a period of consecration under the vow. Judas was also aware at that time of the continuous growth of Jesus' hair. John tells us the Devil put a scheme together for Judas, which proved to be worthy of thirty pieces of silver.

> John 13:2 And, supper being ended, the devil having now put into the heart of Judas Iscariot, Simon's son, to betray him.

> John 13:27 And after the sop Satan entered into him. Then said Jesus unto him, What thou doest, do quickly.

> John 13:30 He, then, having received the sop, went immediately out, and it was night.

> John 13:31 Therefore, when he was gone out, Jesus said, Now is the Son of man glorified, and God is glorified in him.

The preceding scriptures pinpoint the time Judas became confident that he had obtained worthwhile information and a plan for the chief priests. The use of the word "now" in John 13:2 and John 13:31, followed by Judas' immediate exit, are indications that he had arrived at that point. He may have previously met with the chief priest to discuss the Vow of the Nazirite, but to receive the money he needed to be a personal witness to Jesus' statement. Judas knew that the vow had to be uttered and that Jesus would soon reveal to the disciples his commencement and length of consecration. Immediately after Jesus stated the length of the consecration, Judas left the room, because there was no longer any reason to be secretive. Jesus had taken on a period of consecration that would last the rest of his life, and Judas left with confidence that he had just earned his thirty pieces of silver. After Jesus' proclamation, Judas knew that Jesus had placed himself squarely in the hands of the religious authorities. If not for Judas's presence, the length of the period of special consecration would have remained a secret among the disciples. Without knowing the duration of the vow, the chief priests were faced with the prospect that Jesus could end the consecration at any time, and they need him in the midst of the vow while being crucified on the cross. The staged potential violations of the Vow of the Nazirite would taint the sanctity of Jesus before the Jewish community and before God. Now, with the duration confirmed, the trap begins!

Judas had helped the religious leaders' plans reach a point of near perfection. After they had received his report and the high priest had levied the charge of blasphemy, the final stage would be to convince the Roman governor, Pilate, that Jesus had committed a crime worthy of execution under Roman law. The religious leaders and the supporting cast of Jews convinced Pilate that Jesus was guilty of sedition, a crime against the Roman government. Sedition is any speech, conduct, or organized effort that is deemed to subvert the established authority or to incite discontentment to lawful authority. The religious leaders contended that since Jesus implied that he was the Messiah, the coming Davidic king, and the Son of God, he had committed an act of sedition against Roman authority.

John 19:7, 12 The Jews answered, We have a law, and by our law he ought to die, because he made himself the Son of God. And from then Pilate sought to release him; but the Jews cried out, saying, If thou let this man go, thou art not Caesar's friend; whosoever maketh himself a king speaketh against Caesar.

For Jewish leaders of the time, there were serious concerns about Roman rule and an insurgent <u>Zealot</u> movement in <u>Beit Shammai</u> to eject the Romans from <u>Israel</u>. The Romans would not perform execution over violations of <u>Jewish law</u>, and therefore the charge of blasphemy would not have mattered to Pilate. Caiaphas' legal position, therefore, was to establish that Jesus was guilty not only of blasphemy, but also of proclaiming himself the <u>messiah</u>, which was understood as the return of the <u>Davidic</u> king. This would have been an act of sedition and prompted Roman execution.
(Wikipedia, http://en.wikipedia.org/wiki/Caiaphas)

The religious leaders had found a part of the Mosaic Law that perfectly suited their plans and merited the Roman form of capital punishment, crucifixion. As I mentioned earlier, the Jewish form of capital punishment was stoning: an organized group of people casts stones at a convicted individual until he dies. But stoning was not appropriate for the religious leaders' plans. In order for Jesus' death to be beneficial for the whole nation, as Caiaphas, the high priest, had suggested, it was imperative that Jesus be crucified by the Roman government. Caiaphas had convinced the chief priests that they must offer a sacrifice to the monstrous Roman government in order to survive.

> John 11:48–51 If we let him thus alone, all men will believe on him; and the Romans shall come and take away both our place and nation. And one of them, named Caiaphas, being the high priest that same year, said unto them. Ye know nothing at all. Nor consider that it is expedient for us that one man should die for the people, and the whole nation perish not. And this spoke he not of himself, but being high priest the year, he prophesied that Jesus should die for that nation.

However, Judas did not understand the full extent of the trap to be set for Jesus, which included crucifixion:

> Matthew 27:35 Then Judas, who had betrayed him, when he saw that he was condemned, repented, and brought again the thirty pieces of silver to the chief priests and elders. Saying, I have sinned in that I have betrayed innocent blood. And they said, What is that to us? See thou to it. And he cast down the pieces of silver in the temple, and departed, and went and hanged himself.

> In the modern version of this theory it is suggested that Judas, who in common with the other disciples looked for a temporal kingdom of the <u>Messias</u>, did not anticipate the death of <u>Christ</u>, but wished to precipitate a crisis and hasten the hour of triumph, thinking that the arrest would provoke a rising of the people who would set Him free and place Him on the throne. In support of this they point to the fact that, when he found that <u>Christ</u> was condemned and given up to the Romans, he immediately repented of what he had done.
>
> (Catholic Encyclopedia, http://www. newadvent.org/cathen/08539a.htm)

Why was Judas so distraught? The primary cause was the realization that the chief priests and elders had succeeded in getting Jesus condemned under Roman law. He realized that the religious leaders' intentions had been to kill Jesus and that those intentions had become an imminent reality.

It is also not difficult to hypothesize about the strong-willed disciples who had direct knowledge of the advantages of being with Jesus and the great potential for a Jewish revolution. All the factors for a complete and sustained revolution were present around Jesus: a leader of unprecedented power, the multitudes yearning for a new king, and the available resources that could be enhanced by their leader's miracles. All that seemed to be lacking was lighting a little figurative fire under

Jesus to get him to accept the concept of a military revolution. Judas perhaps felt that, as long as Jesus was not touched physically, he would continue in the pacifist mode. He may have thought that if Jesus were taken by his accusers and arrested, he would display more of the anger he showed in the temple when the moneychangers were driven out. But he soon discovered that Jesus had willingly submitted to the condemnation of the chief priests and elders and had offered no defense in the hall of judgment before Pilate. Judas realized that Jesus was being disappointingly true to his words.

The information Judas provided to the chief priest was accepted with such enthusiasm that a plan was set in motion immediately. Within an extremely short period of time, Jesus was on the cross.

Prior to Jesus' arrest in the Garden of Gethsemane, when Jesus announced himself the mob that was with Judas fell to the ground. Shortly afterward, Judas kissed Jesus. Why did Judas have to kiss Jesus to identify him? Why did the men with Judas fall backward to the ground when Jesus approached them? The probable answer is that Jesus had allowed his hair to grow, possibly for several months prior to the week of the Passover. This fact seems to be evident from the scriptural account of his visit to Simon the leper's house.

> Mark 14:3 And being in Bethany in the house of Simon the leper, as he sat eating, there came a woman, having an alabaster box of ointment of spikenard, very precious; and she broke the box, and poured the ointment on his head.

The woman's action of pouring ointment on Jesus' head was a symbolic action based on his statement.

> Matthew 26:7, 10–12 There came unto him a woman having an alabaster box of very precious ointment, and poured it on his head, as he was eating... (10–12) When Jesus understood it he said unto them, Why trouble ye the woman: For she hath wrought a good work upon me. For ye have the poor always with you, but me ye have not always. For in that she hath poured this ointment on my body, she did it for my burial.

However, she did not know her actions would be symbolic until Jesus spoke. Would the woman have just arbitrarily walked up to Jesus and poured oil on his head while he was eating? There was perhaps a truly practical reason why she was compelled to do so. Jesus had allowed his hair to grow freely as part of the Vow of the Nazirite. The woman, who was well acquainted with grooming, exercised her grooming skills on Jesus; she knew just what his hair needed. The fact that she broke the box and poured out the entire content may indicate how much hair the ointment was treating. The woman's actions, though partly motivated by reverence and affection, were full of practicality- she was concerned about Jesus' appearance. The closest resemblance of Jesus' hair today would be the dreadlocks of the Rastafarian movement where the hair is allowed to grow freely into its own pattern; the Rastafarian hairstyle was partly taken from the scriptural account of the Vow of the Nazirite.

> "The wearing of dreadlocks is very closely associated with the movement, though not universal among, or exclusive to, its adherents. Rastas maintain that dreadlocks are supported by Leviticus 21:5 ("They shall not make baldness upon their head, neither shall they shave off the corner of their beard, nor make any cuttings in the flesh") and the Nazirite vow in Numbers 6:5 ("All the days of the vow of his separation there shall no razor come upon his head until the days be fulfilled, in the which he separateth himself unto the Lord …" (http://en.wikipedia.org/wiki/rastafari)

> A nazirite can groom his hair with his hand or scratch his head and needn't be concerned if some hair falls out. However a Nazirite cannot comb his hair since it is a near certainty to pull out some hair.
> (Encyclopedia Biblica, http://en.wikipedia.org/wiki/Nazirite)

> Matthew 26:48–49 Now he that betrayed him gave them a sign, saying whomsoever I shall kiss, that same is he: hold him fast. And forthwith he came to Jesus, and said, Hail, master, and kissed him.

> John 18:48 Jesus, therefore, knowing all
> things that would come upon him, went
> forth, and said unto them, Whom seek ye?
> They answered him, Jesus of Nazareth. Jesus
> said unto them, I am he. And Judas, also,
> who betrayed him, stood with them. As soon
> then, as he had said unto them, I am he, they
> went backward and fell to the ground.

Perhaps the men with Judas were not as informed as
Judas was about Jesus' altered appearance. They were
probably expecting to see the Jesus who walked through
their villages prior to engaging the Vow of the Nazirite.
The appearance of Jesus as the teacher had mostly been
an amiable one but, in the garden they were faced with
a much more aggressive-looking character with a beard
and longer hair. The man who healed the sick out of love
and compassion appeared to have a completely different
nature and seemed ready for a fight. They were looking at
Jesus, who had just concluded an excruciating prayer and
may have been sweaty and appeared agitated.

> Luke 27:44 And being in agony, he prayed
> more earnestly; and his sweat was, as it were,
> great drops of blood falling down to the
> ground.

He was also the one who had recently overturned the
tables in the temple. And they were seeing this change in
appearance at night in the Garden of Gethsemane prior
to an impending fight. The people had witnessed what
Jesus would do while filled with love and compassion,

but no one knew what he would do while filled with anger.

Not only was the prospect of violence present in the minds of the men with Judas but also in the minds of Jesus' disciples prior to their walk to Gethsemane: they had concluded that there was a need for swords and daggers.

> Luke 22:38 And they said, Lord, behold here are two swords. And he said unto them, It is enough.

The disciples evidently knew the essence of Judas's exit from the Last Supper because they went to the Garden of Gethsemane armed. They were very much aware that Judas had left the room and had not returned, and they wondered about Jesus' statement that there was a traitor among them. Jesus had just told them of the inevitability of his death. It was a very emotional moment and not a time for a disciple to exit the room; the Last Supper was a time for the disciples to offer support and reaffirm their commitment to Jesus' ministry. They believed Jesus' words, felt that the betrayal was complete, and prepared for conflict.

It is taught that Jesus prayed in agony for God to remove the bitter cup of crucifixion and death.

> Matthew 26:39, 42, 44 And he went a little further, and fell on his face, and prayed, saying, O my Father, if it be possible, let this cup pass from me; nevertheless, not as I will but as thou will. (42) And he went away again

> the second time, and prayed, saying, O my
> Father, if this cup may not pass away from
> me except I drink it, thy will be done. And he
> left them and went away again, and prayed at
> the third time, saying the same words.

But God refused to alter his plans and release Jesus from his vow and the fulfillment of prophecy (see Isaiah chapter 53 in entirety) through his death. What was the alternative? What would have been the potential subsequent event if Jesus had arisen from prayer free of the cup of crucifixion? The most immediate outcome would have been that the beautiful garden of prayer would have been transformed into a battleground and the place of the beginning of the Jewish/Roman War. The combatants would have been the disciples with the two swords, Peter with his dagger, and Jesus against Judas and the soldiers of the high priest with their swords and the accompanying mob with their sticks. Waiting in the background as reinforcement were Pilate's soldiers, who were loyal to the high priest. Also in the same city was the army of Herod, who was Pilate's enemy and loyal to the Jewish Nation. The battle would have inevitably required the high priest's soldiers to call on Pilate for reinforcement. Word that Roman soldiers were attacking Jews would have evoked great anger and immediate action from Herod's army. Josephus, a first-century Jewish historian, wrote an account of the political atmosphere and tension that existed during the time of Jesus. His account clearly indicates that if a continuous physical altercation had occurred in the garden, it would have been much more than an isolated event.

Luke 23:7 And as soon as he knew that he belonged unto Herod's jurisdiction, he sent him to Herod, who himself also was at Jerusalem at that time.

Luke 23:11 And Herod, with his men of war, treated him with contempt, and mocked him, and arrayed him in a gorgeous robe and sent him again to Pilate.

Josephus identifies this as a period of increasing rebellion, but a contrasting view is that rebellions broke out at the point where rulers changed, famine or other crisis struck, or new rules (especially those affecting religion) were imposed (see Sanders 1996: 28–29). In part, it was peaceful at other times because of the understanding that certain lines could not be crossed with impunity by either side, without problems arising. Potential rebellion was one such line, so was excessively brutal rule or disruption of religious matters. However, the potential for war existed at every moment, because it might take only one officer or member of the public on either side reacting to some small incident which would cause a spark leading to a fire. Hence both Jewish leaders and Roman leaders, acutely aware of this, had strong motives to use the forces at their command to ensure no such small spark could arise and get out of hand.

(Wikipedia, wikipedia.org/wiki/Jesus_in_a_
cultural_and_historical_background)

At the Garden of Gethsemane everyone had molded themselves into a defining role. The religious leader had established an intent to kill Jesus. Judas had established his intent to betray Jesus. The disciples had gathered weapons to show their intention to enter into combat. Jesus, however, was in an agonizing prayer and torn between the role of a military savior or a spiritual savior. Perhaps an influential factor in his agony was the feat of the historical Nazirite, named Samson, who was given a call to consecration and to deliverance:

> Judges 13:5 For, lo, thou shalt conceive, and bear a son, and no razor shall come on his head; for the child shall be a Nazirite unto God from the womb, And he shall begin to deliver Israel out of the hand of the Philistines.

Jesus, the Son of God, was a Nazirite in a period of occupation by a very powerful foreign government similar to that in the time of Samson. The situation in which the Jews found themselves during Jesus' time was truly befitting of the Messiah. The Jewish nation was under the control of the very formidable Roman Empire, whose dominance extended worldwide. The prayer in the Garden of Gethsemane was perhaps not only a moment of tormented petition to God but also a moment of great temptation. It was a moment for the greatest deliverance in Jewish history. Jesus' prayer in the garden was perhaps a request for God to do what he has always done for Israel. He has always provided deliverance.

The disciples did not understand that this prayer was unlike Jesus' previous prayers in the garden. They didn't understand that this moment of prayer would be pivotal in their future interactions with him, nor did they realize that the use of weapons in the garden would jeopardize Jesus' vow of consecration to God. Jesus asked them more than once to watch lest they enter into temptation. He may have been concerned that while he was praying, Judas and the mob would arrive and enter into physical combat with the disciples. If death had occurred among either the disciples or the men with Judas, Jesus would have been in violation of the Vow of the Nazirite. A death in the garden would have replaced the activities at the cross because the violation of being in the presence of the dead would have been evidence enough for the priesthood to sustain an accusation against Jesus.

> Numbers 6:9 If any man die suddenly by him, and he hath defiled the head of his consecration, then he shall shave his head in the days of his cleansing, on the seventh day shall he shave it.

The priesthood would not have offered him the rite of cleansing or the opportunity to end the vow at the temple. The time frame for the crucifixion would probably have been after seven days of incarceration in the Roman jail, after which the priests would have declared Jesus unclean.

Though an outbreak of fighting did not occur in the Garden of Gethsemane, a single act of violence did occur when Judas and the crowd with him came forward to arrest Jesus. A disciple cut off the ear of a servant of the high priest, but Jesus quickly mended it to prevent any escalation of violence.

> Matthew 26:51 And, behold, one of those who were with Jesus stretched out his hand, and drew his sword, and struck a servant of the high priest's and smote off his ear.

> Luke 22:51 And Jesus answered, and said, Permit ye thus far, And he touched his ear, and healed him.

Jesus' steadfast commitment to his own teaching and to the will of God was crucial to controlling the situation in the Garden of Gethsemane. It is very possible that the healing of the servant's ear took away much of the mob's passion for violence. Perhaps many of them had never witnessed a miracle by Jesus and were in awe. Because of his disposition, the religious leaders were forced to carry out their scheme to discredit and kill Jesus on the cross.

# CHAPTER 4:
## AT THE CROSS

Upon hearing Judas' report from the Last Supper, the religious leaders began to arrange the trap for Jesus around the confinements of the Vow of the Nazirite. Since it had restrictions on being in the presence of the dead, it was perfect for the Roman method of capital punishment by crucifixion, and the religious leaders planned to include two thieves. But death was not the religious leaders' final expectation; a teacher or prophet who is condemned to death with a good name becomes a martyr to his followers. Thus Calvary was especially prepared to destroy Jesus' name and legacy and to discourage or threaten his present and future followers. Prophets, priests, and great teachers were esteemed very highly by all Jews. Some had ranked Jesus among the greatest:

> Matthew 16:13–14 When Jesus came into the borders of Caesarea Philippi, he asked his disciples, saying, Who do men say that I, son of man, am? And they said, some say that thou are John the Baptist. Some Elijah and others Jeremiah, or one of the prophets.

However, some took a contrasting view that aided the plans of the religious leaders, who needed a pool of doubters from which to recruit a crowd opposing Jesus in the Judgment Hall and at the cross. Since the trial and execution of Jesus were during the festivities of the Passover, there was an abundance of people who were probably willing to participate for pay.

> John 7:12 And there was much murmuring among the people concerning him; for some said, He is a good man; others said, Nay but he deceiveth the people.

One of the religious leaders' preliminary steps in preparation for the Crucifixion was to get Barabbas as a candidate for the customary release of a prisoner during the Passover.

> The penalty for Barabbas' crime was death by <u>crucifixion</u>, but according to the four canonical gospels and the <u>Gospel of Peter</u> there was a prevailing Passover custom in Jerusalem that allowed or required Pilate, the *praefectus* or governor of Judaea, to commute one prisoner's death sentence by popular acclaim, and the "crowd" (*ochlos*)—which has become "the <u>Jews</u>" and "the multitude" in some translations were offered a choice of whether to have Barabbas or Jesus Christ released from Roman custody.

(Encyclopedia Biblica, http://en.wikipedia.org/wiki/Barabbas)

Surely Barabbas was not Pilate's choice as a candidate for release:

> In books and movies, Barabbas is usually depicted as an evil criminal. But he may have actually been a freedom fighter in the Jewish resistance to the Romans. Evidence for this can be found at Mark 15:7, which says that he was in prison because he had taken part in a recent uprising. In fact, some biblical scholars think that he was an important rebel leader. If so, this would explain why the crowd shouted for his release, because any leader in the fight against the hated Romans would be very popular with the common people. (http://www.gospel-mysteries.net/barabbas.html)

Each of Barabbas' criminal charges in historical record was a crime that led him to capital punishment by crucifixion: robbery, murder, and sedition. Pilate had the responsibility of keeping the peace between the Jews and the Romans, and he was well known for swift trials leading to executions. A seditionist, whose crimes would have been known to Rome, would have been primary on Pilate's list for execution.

> Mark 15:7 And there was one named Barabbas, who lay bound with them that

> had made insurrection with him, who had
> committed murder in the insurrection.

It seems from Mark 15:7 that Barabbas was a leader of a band of insurrectionists. It is then curious that Pilate decided to give such a rebel the slightest hope of being released. That hope, no matter how slight, would be an insult to the hard work of his soldiers in capturing Barabbas. The only conceivable reason for Pilate's action was to display Barabbas's capture before the people, believing that the people were so loyal to Rome that they would do the right thing for the Jewish-Roman relationship. Or, is it conceivable that the religious leaders convinced Pilate that Barabbas offered such a stark contrast to Jesus that the people would surely choose Jesus? But Pilate did not realize that he was an unsuspecting player in the Crucifixion scheme. If the people had chosen Jesus for release, Pilate would have been free to execute Barabbas. The scriptures say that the people called out Barabbas' name and, per the custom, were normally granted their wish. However, it seems highly unlikely that any ruler would release a man who might come back the next day to assassinate him.

There is a strange irony in the chief priests and elders' request for Barabbas's release. Caiaphas, the high priest, counseled the priests and elders that one man (Jesus) should die to save the Jewish nation. His counsel was a result of the fear of a Roman takeover of the Jewish provinces and the removal of the Jews from positions of authority. But Rome was entertaining an invasion because of the rise in revolts led by Jewish insurgents such as Barabbas. How is it possible that the religious leaders wanted Barabbas to be released and continue his war against Rome and at the same time wanted Jesus to die to ease the tension with Rome? Can Caiaphas' counsel really be considered a true assessment of his and his colleagues' intent?

The religious leaders used the most holy time of the year, the Passover, as the perfect backdrop for a most unholy act: the formation of the cross trap. The religious authorities knew that once they had succeeded in getting Barabbas to be a candidate for release, they had to put forth a very persuasive effort to convince Pilate to release him rather than Jesus. A strong point of persuasion was the crowd that had assembled outside of the Judgment Hall.

> John 18:28–29 Then led they Jesus from Caiaphas unto the hall of judgment; and it was early. And they themselves went not into the judgment hall, lest they should be defiled; but that they might eat the Passover. Pilate then went out unto them, and said, What accusation bring ye against this man?

If the religious leaders had gone into the Judgment Hall to meet with Pilate, the crowd with them would not have been allowed to enter, and the voices of the religious leaders alone may not have been enough to persuade Pilate. They had planned the meeting during the Passover, which prohibited them from entering and which forced Pilate to come out to hear the people.

Lest they should be defiled. These Jewish leaders, filled with the hate of Christ, and ready to secure his judicial murder by the foulest means, were yet so scrupulous that they would not enter the house of a Gentile lest they should be defiled (see De 16:4), so that they would not be able to eat the Passover. The Pharisees held that contact with a Gentile, or to enter his house was a source of defilement. Hence, this deputation of the Sanhedrin waited without, and Pilate went out unto them to ascertain their business. Men can be very religious and yet great sinners.
(Biblog.com,      http://bible.cc/john/18-28. htm)

Pilate was overwhelmed by the voices in the crowd and the religious leaders' threats. Who were the people in the crowd? Very few people attend a court hearing out of mere curiosity. The vast majority of attendees at a trial are there for the benefit of a close acquaintance or a relative, or for educational or business purposes. The crowd at the Judgment Hall probably consisted of friends and relatives of Barabbas and comrades in the insurgency. To enhance the number of attendees, the religious leaders probably did not hesitate to use their most persuasive tool—money. Pilate considered the Jews he saw in the Judgment Hall to be representative of the majority. They could not have been low-income commoners, whose opinions Pilate could easily dismiss. They may have been members of the Sanhedrin Court and others who appeared to be of some prominence in Jewish society. The people in the crowd had to be people upon whom Pilate would infer the right to debate before him, and especially so in a case of capital punishment.

The success the religious leaders achieved in the Judgment Hall before Pilate was the final act leading to the reality of seeing Jesus on the cross. Pilate later ordered the soldiers to scourge Jesus. This book maintains that the activities leading to and surrounding the Crucifixion are intertwined; thus no event, such as the scourging, should be view as a solitary one. Considered alone, it seems Pilate had the intention of discouraging Jesus' execution: scourging was a Roman form of punishment. However, if one studies closer the laws and practices concerning the Vow of the Nazirite and other vows in the Bible, a question arises: was this scourging part of a diabolical scheme to insult the priestly character of Jesus? If a Nazirite failed to complete his vow, he was subject to lashes.

> If a Nazirite fails in fulfilling these three obligations there may be consequences. All or part of the person's time as a Nazirite may need to be repeated. Furthermore, the person may be obligated to bring sacrifices, and, in certain circumstances, suffer a penalty of lashes
> (Wikipedia Biblica.org, http://en.wikipedia.org/wiki/Nazirite)

At first view the scourging was, as some writers indicate, a hopeful deterrent to crucifixion in Pilate's mind. But if the scourging is viewed in conjunction with the other events of the cross trap, one can see that all of the events surrounding the Crucifixion were an attack on the priestly character of Jesus. The Book of John shows that the lashes were given just prior to the mockery with the robe and crown of thorns; John seems to indicate that they were related activities.

> John 19:15 Then Pilate, therefore, took Jesus, and scourged him. And the soldiers platted a crown of thorns, and put it on his head, and they put on him a purple robe. And said, Hail, King of the Jews! And they smote him with their hands. Pilate, therefore, went forth again and saith unto them, Behold, I bring him forth to you, that ye may know I find not fault in him. Then came Jesus forth, wearing the crown of thorns, and the purple robe. And Pilate saith, Behold the man!

If Pilate's intent was to discourage the Crucifixion, why did he allow Barabbas to stand before the people as a strong warrior willing to fight for the destiny of the Jews and then parade Jesus before the people as an embarrassment? Pilate's action of displaying Jesus in such a manner was evidence that he endorsed the mockery. Judging by the soldiers' actions and Pilate's subtle stamp of approval, it is not surprising that the chief priests and elders were successful in getting Barabbas released.

The scriptures states that during the procession to the cross, the soldiers asked a man named Simon to bear Jesus' cross.

> Matthew 27:31–32 And after they had mocked him, they took the robe off from him, and put his own raiment on him, and led him away to crucify him. And as they came out, they found a man of Cyrene, Simon by name; him they compelled to bear his cross.

Some teach that it was an honor for Simon to do that for the condemned Savior to ease his suffering. But why were the soldiers concerned with the suffering of a man who was condemned to death? Some teach and others have graphically dramatized in film that the soldiers brutally scourged Jesus before his walk to Calvary. If so, is it logical to believe that the people who were responsible for the beating would also be concerned about easing his suffering on the way to Calvary? Were they not the ones who had made the crown of thorns and would eventually nail him to the cross? Historically it has been considered a relief for a condemned man to die before his scheduled execution. There was no one chosen to take the crosses of the thieves. Perhaps there is another reason for Simon to bear the cross. Could it have been that the priesthood wanted Jesus to be strong enough to survive on the cross longer than the thieves? Pilate, in his questionable effort to discourage the crucifixion, might have allowed a scourging at a degree greater than the religious leaders had expected. This scourging was counterproductive to the trap they had planned. With Simon carrying his cross, Jesus would potentially be able to retain more of his body fluids and strength, and the assistance expedited Jesus' walk to Calvary. The religious leaders were also probably concerned that Jesus' struggle with the cross would augment public sympathy, which could eventually lead to public outcry against the Crucifixion. Increased public sentiment would be counterproductive to their desire to bring shame upon Jesus.

The scriptures state that there was a container of vinegar and gall at the foot of the cross from which Jesus was offered a drink while on the cross. Was it customary for a container of vinegar and gall, or any other drink or nourishment, to be provided to condemned men who are expected to die? Was the purpose of the vinegar and gall to ease a man's suffering after nails had been driven through his hands and feet? Considering the fact that the Jews later requested of Pilate that the legs of the condemned men be broken to expedite death, the container of vinegar and gall was in direct contrast. Why would there be a drink or comfort for someone whom the religious leaders would wish to die before the day was done? Who brought the container of vinegar and gall to the Crucifixion? It is hard to imagine a soldier walking with Jesus and the thieves and also carrying a container of vinegar. Since Jesus was turned over to the high priest by Pilate to be put to death, it is logical to believe that the high priest, the chief priests, and the elders knew what items would be at the cross. It seems logical that the container was placed there by them or one of their servants. The liquid was obviously meant only for Jesus since the scriptures give no account of a drink being offered to the thieves. The container of vinegar was an integral part of the trap and directly associated with the Vow of the Nazirite. The religious leaders knew that Jesus had to refrain from drinking the fruit of the vine or any vinegar or any other product from the grape. They knew also that a man hanging on the cross all day would soon long for a refreshing drink of any kind. They expected the natural need for survival to dominate Jesus's mind more than did his commitment to his vow. Jesus proved them wrong and maintained both his mental acuity and his commitment: he refused to drink.

> Matthew 27:34 They gave him vinegar to drink, mingled with gall; and when he had tasted it, he would not drink.

> Mark 15:23 And they gave him to drink wine mingled with myrrh; but he received it not.

Other gospel writers also say that Jesus received the vinegar and gall but did so only to taste it. After he tasted it, he knew it was a forbidden drink and refused it.

The hill of Calvary or Golgotha was staged in recognition of Jesus' commitment to the Vow of the Nazirite. The historical pictures and the scriptures clearly depict that Jesus was in the center of two dying men. And, as part of the key to the trap, the two thieves were probably feeble and starved.

> John 19:18 Where they crucified him, and two others with him, on either side one, and Jesus in the center.

> Luke 23:33 And when they were come to the place which is called Calvary, there they

> crucified him, and the malefactors, one on
> the right hand, and the other on the left.

If Pilate turned Jesus over to the chief priests to be crucified, who chose the two thieves? Were they also turned over to the chief priests for execution? Is it conceivable that Pilate had scheduled their public execution in Jerusalem during the festivities of the Passover? That would surely have been detrimental to Rome's efforts to maintain peace with the Jews. As with the vinegar and gall, the chief priests knew who and what would be at the cross, and each person and item was there for a specific purpose.

If either of the two men had died before Jesus, Jesus would have failed to keep his vow to his Father. If they both died before Jesus, there would have been further confirmation that Jesus had defiled himself by being in the company of the dead. The religious leaders knew that he would be helpless to change his plight while hanging on the cross. The chief priests were, of course, not willing to offer him the opportunity for the cleansing the vow required. Who would shave off Jesus' hair while he was on the cross so he could conform to the vow? The expectation was that he would die as a vow breaker and thus a lawbreaker who could not possibly be the Son of God. If Jesus was to be the Messiah, or the Lamb of God, for the salvation of man, then he would be a blemished sacrifice, bruised and spoiled—a mockery before God.

# CHAPTER 5:
# CONTROLLING DEATH

> John 19:30 When Jesus, therefore, had
> received the vinegar, he said, It is finished,
> and he bowed his head, and gave up the
> ghost.

Since Jesus refused to drink the vinegar and gall, which would have been in violation of the Vow of the Nazirite, the religious leaders had only one part of the vow to work with: the violation of being in the presence of the dead. They soon realized that Jesus was also uncooperative in manifesting that particular violation; he hung his head and appeared to succumb to death before the thieves. The religious leaders found themselves at a moment of desperation and needed to use their final hope for success in discrediting Jesus. The scriptures say that the Jews petitioned Pilate to have the legs of the condemned men broken because the Crucifixion was taking place during the preparation for the Sabbath. They told Pilate they did not want the men on the cross during the Sabbath because it was an important day of joyous celebrations:

> John 19:31 The Jews, therefore, because it
> was the preparation, that the bodies would
> not remain upon the cross on the Sabbath
> day (for that Sabbath day was an high day),
> besought Pilate that their legs might be
> broken, and that they might be taken away.

But these leaders had known from the beginning on what day Jesus would be crucified; after all, Pilate had turned Jesus over to them. If they had been truly concerned about the Sabbath from the beginning, the breaking of the legs would have been included in the initial planning and there would have been no need to petition Pilate. They made the request when they found themselves needing to control the visual perception of the time of death.

The soldiers received instruction from Pilate to break the legs of Jesus and the two thieves.

> ... the legs of the person executed were
> broken or shattered with an iron club, an act
> called *crurifragium* which was also frequently
> applied without crucifixion to slaves. This
> act hastened the death of the person but was
> also meant to <u>deter</u> those who observed the
> crucifixion from committing offenses.
> (Wikipedia, http://en.wikipedia.org/wiki/
> Crucifixion)

> In Roman-style crucifixion, the condemned
> took days to die slowly from suffocation—
> caused by the condemned's blood-supply

slowly draining away to a quantity insufficient to supply the required oxygen to vital organs. The dead body was left up for <u>vultures</u> and other birds to consume. The goal of Roman crucifixion was not just to kill the criminal, but also to mutilate and dishonour the body of the condemned. In ancient tradition, an honourable death required burial; leaving a body on the cross, so as to mutilate it and prevent its burial was a grave dishonour. (Wikipedia, http://en.wikipedia.org/wiki/Crucifixion)

The Bible gives specific information on the arrangement of the crosses and indicates the soldiers' view of the crosses, stating that a malefactor was on the right side of Jesus and one was on the left side.

John 19:18 Where they crucified him, and two others with him, on either side one, and Jesus in the center.

Luke 23:33 And when they were come to the place which is called Calvary, there they crucified him, and the malefactors, one on the right hand, and the other on the left.

Both the scene and the soldiers at the scene were under the religious leaders' control. If things were done in a sequential order, the legs of one of the thieves would have been broken, then Jesus' legs, and then those of the other thief. Jesus, being in the middle, should have been the second person regardless of where the soldiers began. But the soldiers broke the thieves' legs before approaching Jesus.

> John 19:32–33 Then came the soldiers, and broke the legs of the first, and of the other who was crucified with him. But when they came to Jesus, and saw that he was already dead, they broke not his legs.

The scriptures imply that the soldiers worked in concert and went together to each cross; therefore, they came to Jesus together. Logically speaking, the one whose legs were broken first would be expected to die first and the rest would die in order. With the soldiers controlling the visual perception of the rate of death, Jesus would have been the last to have his legs broken and presumably the last to die. The religious leaders could then record for history that Jesus had violated the Vow of the Nazirite by being in the company of the dead. He would have been reduced to a vow breaker who truly could not be the Son of God in the eyes of the doubters. Since the Crucifixion was held within range of the city, there would be a multitude of witnesses to this visual perception of the time of death. The robust Jesus was surely expected to live longer than the feeble, possibly starved men who had been selected especially for the Crucifixion.

John 19:30 says that Jesus gave up the ghost or spirit. The same writer says that Jesus received the vinegar and gall. It is obvious that these scriptures were written from observation at a distance because it is written in other scriptures that Jesus tasted the mixture that was offered him and refused it.

> John 19:30 When Jesus, therefore, had received the vinegar, he said, It is finished; and he bowed his head, and gave up the spirit.

The following chapter will highlight the important difference between observation and what was actually happening. Jesus' death was very premature, which evokes discussions among scholars today about the physical effects of the crucifixion that eventually led to his death. However, the visual perception of a premature death was crucial in the saga of God against the forces of evil working through the religious authorities to discredit the Son of God.

# CHAPTER 6:
## GOD TRUMPS THE TRAP

Mark 15; 33–34 And when the sixth hour was come, there was darkness over the whole land until the ninth hour. And at the ninth hour Jesus cried with a loud voice, saying, Eloi, Eloi, lama sabachthani? Which is, being interpreted, My God, My God, why hast thou forsaken me?

In the preceding scriptures Jesus was again, as in the Garden of Gethsemane, agonizing over God's response to his plight. He knew that the activities around and the setting of the cross were designed to produce violations of the Law. Jesus had done all he physically could to keep his commitment; he refused the drink of vinegar, and he refrained from miraculously coming down from the cross even though he was the Son of God and in the presence of dying men. Without some form of intervention from God, being in the presence of the dead was inevitable. Jesus garnered hope from the sixth hour to the ninth hour during which darkness covered the earth. This was the period when one would expect God to unleash his anger by opening up the earth to swallow Jesus' enemies or sending down fire to devour them. Jesus had commented to the disciples in the Garden of Gethsemane about his ability to summon angels to his rescue.

> Matthew 26:53 Thinkest thou that I cannot now pray to my Father, and he shall presently give me more than twelve legions of angels.

But all Jesus could see was three hours of a gloomy acknowledgment of his plight by his Father. And as the darkness lifted on the ninth hour, he realized there would be no dramatic rescue and seemingly no recourse to being trapped between two dying thieves. Jesus then immediately cried out, "Eloi, Eloi, lama sabachthani" or "My God, My God, Why hast thou forsaken me?" These words rang out because he was able to gather enough strength to say them aloud in frustration; however, he may have said many more words in silent prayer prior to the outburst. This was not a cry to remove the cup of suffering, because Jesus had already accepted his fate after the prayer in the Garden of Gethsemane. This was a different plea because of the formidable cross trap. At this point of desperation, Jesus had the power to come down from the cross because he was the Son of God. But he was firm in his commitment of obedience to the Father to the death.

God had arranged for Jesus' death to precede those of the thieves and to do so by infallible proof. The scriptures say that Jesus gave up the ghost (spirit). Some believe the statement literally because of the belief that the act was a symbol of his power over life and death. Also, Jesus had taught in his Good Shepherd message that he indeed had such power to give up his life and then take it up again.

> John 10:17–18 Therefore doth my Father love me, because I lay down my life, that I might take it again. No man taketh it from me but I lay it down of myself, I have power to lay it down, and I have power to take it again. This commandment have I received of my Father.

However, greater than the power over life and death was Jesus' obedience to the will of God, which he exhibited both throughout his ministry and on the cross. It must be understood that his death had to come wholly through an act of his executioners and that God had arranged for such an act. When Pilate granted the petition for the legs of the condemned men to be broken, the soldiers perceived that Jesus was already dead, a perception they achieved visually. A soldier pierced him in the side with a spear that released blood and water. Then Joseph of Arimathea went to Pilate to request the body of Jesus for burial.

> Mark 15:43–45 Joseph of Arimathea, an honorable counselor, who also waited for the kingdom of God, came, and went in boldly unto Pilate, and asked for the body of Jesus. And Pilate marveled if he was already dead, and, calling unto him the centurion, he asked him whether he had been any while dead.

> And when he knew it from the centurion, he
> gave the body to Joseph.

What was it that convinced Pilate of Jesus' death? His reaction to the news of Jesus' early death showed that, even after their legs were broken, men were expected to cling to life a little longer. But Pilate was convinced by the centurion's report that a soldier had pierced Jesus with a spear and a massive amount of blood and body fluid had been released; he knew that no man could survive after being pierced with the Roman spear while hanging on the cross. The release of the massive amount of blood and body fluid offered undeniable evidence that Jesus was dead—and had died first. Any person of medicine then, now, and in the future could safely conclude that the massive expulsion of blood and body fluid would produce a much more rapid death then the breaking of legs. The Bible does not indicate which of Jesus' sides was pierced, but in considering God's response to the almost perfect trap, it could well be assumed that the piercing was done on the left side where the heart is located. This would be consisted with Revelation 5:6. It is the piercing of Jesus' side that is the testimonial in heaven even though much focus has been on the nail prints in his hands and feet.

> Revelation 5:6 And I beheld, and lo, in the
> midst of the throne and of the four living
> creatures, and in the midst of the elders,
> stood a Lamb as though it had been slain,
> having seven horns and seven eyes, which are

the seven spirits of God sent forth into all the world.

John describes the Savior as a Lamb that had been slain. What would be more graphic evidence of a slaughter than a large gash in the left side near the heart? If John was looking at the Lamb (Christ) while he stood among others, the most noticeable bodily damage would be the gash in his side. It would take much closer scrutiny and perhaps even touch to determine that there were wounds in the hands and feet.

The gospel writers' statements that Jesus gave up the spirit or ghost were statements of observation, not of actual facts. Neither writer had conclusive proof of death; instead, they observed what were commonly accepted in their time as the signs of death. The scriptures say that Jesus hung his head, and one can easily assume that there was no outward evidence of breathing. But there should be a consensus agreement that the piercing by a Roman spear and the expulsion of blood and water would bring a very rapid and sure death; the Roman spear was designed especially for that purpose. The Book of John is the only book of the gospel that tells that the soldiers broke the legs of the thieves and that one soldier pierced Jesus' side with the spear. Immediately after describing the event, John mentions two scriptures of prophecy that say Jesus' legs would not be broken and that they shall look upon him whom they pierced:

> John 19:33–37 But when they came to Jesus, and saw that he was dead already, they broke not his legs. But one of the soldiers, with a

> spear, pierced his side, and immediately came there out blood and water. And he that saw it bore witness, and his witness is true; and he knoweth that he saith true, that ye might believe. For these things were done, that the scriptures should be fulfilled, A bone of him shall not be broken. And, again, another scripture saith, They shall look upon him whom they pierced.

John 19:37 is indicating that it was the piercing that ushered in death for Jesus, an early death at the hands of his executioners. It is obvious from the scriptures that the nails in the hands and feet did not bring on this early death. The scriptures show that crucifixion sometimes required additional measures to bring on death, such as the breaking of the legs. Also, since the Crucifixion was such a public execution, everyone who watched could see the long Roman spear being thrust through Jesus' body. The visual effect was clear, dramatic, and undeniable. The Roman soldier's action offered a strong point of discussion for any legal argument among the Jewish leaders about the time of Jesus' death. There were others, such as Joseph of Arimathea, who were disciples of Jesus and were able to counter the post-Crucifixion spin by the religious leaders, who wanted to portray Jesus as one who broke a consecrated vow to God. If Jesus had not been pierced by the spear, the truth of his death and resurrection would never have been confirmed by infallible proof. If he had risen the third day as a man who was only nailed to the cross, the stories of his resurrection would not have been impactful, then or now. Whether or not he actually died would have been a topic of many passionate debates from that day forward.

The chief priest had arranged for the Crucifixion to take place just before the Sabbath. That meant that if the plan had gone well, Jesus would have remained on the cross until the third day because no work would have been done on the Sabbath. The high priest had planned for the cross to be the keeper of Jesus' body until the third day, when Jesus said he would rise.

> ...The dead body was left up for <u>vultures</u> and other birds to consume. The goal of Roman crucifixion was not just to kill the criminal, but also to mutilate and dishonour the body of the condemned.
> (Wikipedia,http://en.wikipedia.org/wiki/Historicity_of_Jesus)

The religious leaders were well aware of the Roman method of crucifixion that included the mutilation of the body, and its removal after several days. They savored the thought of the Roman crucifixion as their answer to everything about Jesus, including his claim to be able to rise from the dead after three days.

If the trap had been successful, the priesthood would have gathered the people back to the cross on the third day to make a mockery of Jesus. At that time they would have proclaimed that Jesus violated the Vow of the Nazirite to God in the presence of a multitude of witnesses. The soldiers and the priest would have testified that Jesus drank the fruit of the vine. A soldier would have testified that he broke Jesus' legs much later than those of the thieves. They would all have been witnesses to Jesus' death after the two thieves had died. But the piercing of his body with the spear nullified the religious leaders' efforts to control the visual time of death. It also made it possible for Jesus to be removed from the cross before the thieves and before the Sabbath.

Their trap had completely disintegrated: Jesus refused to drink the vinegar and gall; he would not come down off the cross even though he had the power to as the Son of God; he was pierced, unexpectedly, with the spear, which sealed the time of death. God used deception to defeat his enemy as he had done in Jewish history, such as during Gideon's war. If Jesus had not cried out and hung his head, the religious leaders would not have petitioned Pilate for the legs to be broken, and had they not made such a petition, the soldiers would not have approached Jesus with the spear, which subsequently led to the piercing. If the onlookers observed the soldiers' actions from afar, they would have had a different perception as the soldiers approached the condemned men. The breaking of the legs would have produced a flow of blood that was not easily discernible at a distance. The Roman soldiers would have recoiled slightly to avoid a splattering of blood. In contrast, the piercing produced a massive expulsion of body fluids as the spear was withdrawn. The soldiers' reaction in that case would have been similar to a dash for cover from enemy fire.

The religious leaders had arranged for the Crucifixions to be a widespread public event during the heavily populated time of the Passover festivities. There were thus many eyewitness accounts of it. The time of the piercing and Jesus' death were visibly discernible from a distance.

The time of death of the thieves was also discernible from a distance as their bodies ceased to move. It could then be concluded with infallible proof that Jesus died first and was not in close proximity to dead bodies while he lived. This saga of death went down to the wire.

The scriptures say that Joseph of Arimathea went boldly before Pilate and begged for Jesus' body, which he did through the inspiration of God. Pilate, needing to appear neutral in the Crucifixion drama, could not refuse the earnest plea of a man as honorable as Joseph of Arimathea, and he released the body to him in opposition to the high priest's plan. Thus the people saw Jesus being removed from the cross before the thieves. The chief priests and others were obviously upset at Pilate's decision and approached him with angry words, making him a principal in the initial plan of Crucifixion that failed to discredit Jesus. The only recourse available after Jesus was taken down from the cross was to deal with the issue of the Resurrection:

> Matthew 27:62–66 Now the next day that followed the day of preparation, the chief priest and Pharisees came together unto Pilate. Saying, Sir, we remember that that deceiver said, while he was yet alive, After three days I will rise again. Command, therefore, the sepulchre be made sure until the third day, lest his disciples come by night, and steal him away, and say unto the people He is risen from the dead, so the last error shall be worst than the first. Pilate said unto them, Ye have a watch, go your way, make it

> as sure as you can. So they went, and made
> the sepulchre sure, sealing the stone, and
> setting a watch.

The conversation between the chief priest, the Pharisees, and Pilate showed they believed there had been an error. How could there have been an error if Jesus was condemned, went to the cross, and died? What more were they expecting? It is obvious from their conversation that the religious leaders had included the Crucifixion as part of a more intricate plan—and that plan had completely unraveled. They seem to implicate Pilate's organization as the reason for the failure. Was it because the soldier pierced Jesus' body with the spear? The chief priest impressed upon Pilate that it was his responsibility to correct that error by having the tomb sealed and guards placed at the entrance. Pilate concurred with the chief priests and the Pharisees and ordered the tomb sealed as securely as possible. Neither the religious leaders nor Pilate understood that they were trying to counter God's plan; they viewed their failure as an "error." They found themselves dependent upon the grave to be their ally and a cover for this error. But the grave was unable to cooperate, and the religious leaders found themselves needing another cover to explain the opened grave and the Resurrection. The high priest and his counsels bribed the soldiers who guarded the entrance to the tomb into saying that Jesus' body had been taken from the grave by his disciples.

> Matthew 28:11–15 Now when they were
> going, behold, some of the watch came into

the city, and showed unto the high priest everything that was done. And when they were assembled with the elders, and had taken counsel, they gave much money unto the soldiers, saying, say ye, His disciples came by night, and stole him away while we slept. And if this come to the Governor's ear, we will persuade him, and secure you. So they took the money, and did as they were taught; and this saying is commonly reported among the Jews until this day.

The chief priests, the elders, and the high priest knew "nothing at all," as Caiaphas had said to them in his speech about Jesus being a sacrifice for the nation. They were still focused on the manhood of Jesus so much that they did not wait for the whole truth. Jesus' resurrection had not only opened his grave; there were reports of other people once dead walking the streets.

Matthew 27:52–53 And the graves were opened; and many bodies of the saints that slept were raised, And came out of the graves after his resurrection, and went into the holy city, and appeared unto many.

It is curious that in all the scriptures of the synoptic gospels there is no mention of any man among the scribes, the Pharisees, or the entire priesthood who was bold enough to come forward to warn the religious leaders of the possible futility of their actions. In the book of Acts,

Gamaliel, a Pharisee and teacher of the Law, warned his comrades of their intended actions.

> Acts 5:34–35, 38–39 Then stood there up one in the council, a Pharisee, named Gamaliel, a teacher of the law, held in reputation among all the people, and commanded to put the apostles forth a little space. And said unto them, Ye men of Israel, take heed to yourselves what ye intend to do as touching these men. And now I say unto you, Refrain from these men, and let them alone; for if this counsel or this work be of men, it will come to nothing. But if it be of God, ye cannot overthrow it, lest perhaps ye be found even to fight against God.

The continuous efforts of the chief priests and elders to seek alternatives to all that was thwarting their plan may be an indication of the immense power they had acquired under the Roman government. Pilate was reported to have been a ruthless governor, and perhaps the religious leaders took on some of the characteristics of Pilate, their benefactor.

# CHAPTER 7:
# THE NAZIRITE'S CHARACTER

The most convincing way to prove that a man is a false teacher is to have him act contrary to his own teachings. The religious leaders wanted Jesus to appear contrary— contrary to religious laws, Roman laws, his own teaching and in conflict with the people. The constant mockery, cursing, and accusations against him that began at the Judgment Hall and continued at the cross were designed to goad him into a negative reaction.

During Jesus' ministry, the Jews were uncertain of the character required of the Messiah who was expected to lead them against the Roman occupation. Many of Jesus' followers expected him to exhibit a warrior's attitude and mount a horse with his sword drawn to lead the deliverance of the Jews. The twelve disciples even wrestled with the idea of a passive Savior who would lead by way of the cross. But upon entering the consecration of the Vow of the Nazirite, Jesus entered into a set of defined character traits that were expected of the consecrated individual. The vow gave the people a standard of character by which to measure his behavior. During the show of mocking and railing, Jesus was not only the keeper of a vow but also the icon for his own teachings:

> Matthew 5:44–45, 48 For I say unto you, Love your enemies, bless them that curse you, do good to them that hate you, and pray for them who despitefully use you, and persecute you. That ye may be the sons of your Father, who is in heaven; for he maketh his sun to rise on the evil and on the good, and sendeth rain on the just and on the unjust. Be ye, therefore, perfect, even as your Father, who is in heaven, is perfect.

When Simon relieved him of the cross during the procession to the cross, Jesus was free to interact verbally with the crowd. He was free to match curse with curse and unleash his own barrage of accusations and complaints. Even though Jesus was the Son of God, the scriptures say that he was capable of feeling the same inner passions of disgust and anger as any other man.

> Hebrew 4:15 For we have not an high priest who cannot be touched with the feeling of our infirmities, but was in all points tempted like as we are, yet without sin.

But Jesus' demeanor was not determined by the actions of those around him; he maintained his integrity to the cross and unto death. Author and pastor Brian Schwertley best described the behavior of the people at the cross in his writing "The Heart of the Gospel: Gethsemane to the

Burial of Christ, Chapter 22, the Reaction to the Death of Christ and the Accompanying Phenomenon" (The Covenant Reformation Press, 2007, schwertley@mwwb. net):

> "…This crowd (or at least the majority of it) had come to Golgotha to take great pleasure in the suffering, humiliation and death of Jesus. These were the Jews of Jerusalem who followed the lead of their religious and political leaders who rejected Christ as a pretender, a false prophet, a blasphemer and sorcerer. They were not shocked by the scene of the crucifixion but rather relished it. They looked upon the bleeding Savior with smiles on their faces, with mocking eyes and scornful lips. They spent their time laughing and heaping insults and derision upon the Mediator. They all exulted over the pain and agony of the defenseless Man who hung before them. As far as they were concerned the Nazarene was now defeated, finished and would soon be forgotten.

Jesus, the Son of God, was endowed with righteousness that is seen throughout the scriptures. Jesus, the prophet, the teacher, and the Nazirite priest, was perceived to be righteous through his character and interactions with the people. The people at the cross, who were initially heavily influenced by the high priest and the other religious authorities, were able to make independent judgment of his character and righteousness. For example, after

Jesus appeared to have died, the centurion made a public exclamation:

> Luke 23:46–47 And when Jesus had cried with a loud voice, he said, Father, into thy hands I commend my spirit, and, having said thus, he gave up the spirit. Now when the centurion saw what was done, he glorified God, saying, Certainly this was a righteous man.

The centurion's reaction was not the result of a singular moment but of the culmination of Jesus' responses to the events of his execution. Jesus complained not. He arranged accommodation for his mother, he asked God to forgive his accusers, and his focus was always toward heaven. The crowd neither heard cursing nor saw any display of anger.

> Roman historians tell us that victims usually filled the air with curses at this point, cursing the soldiers, the onlookers, the gods. But, as the other two victims presumably did this, notice what Jesus cries out (read vs. 34: "but …" ). Amazingly, his desire was not for retaliation for what was being done to him, but rather for God's forgiveness of the ones doing it to him!! This is the first glimpse of the spiritual significance of his crucifixion— it is connected to Jesus' concern for our forgiveness.

(Xenos Christian Fellowship, John 19, The Crucifixion of Jesus. http://www.xenos.org/teachings/nt/john/gary/john19-1.htm)

What if Jesus had turned his focus earthward and decided he did not want to participate further in his crucifixion? What would have been the immediate aftermath if he had decided to come down from the cross? The primary focus of the cross trap was to destroy Jesus' name in the minds of the people and in history. There had been many men of God who had been associated with miracles after prayerful communication with God; however, all had been subject to death. John the Baptist was killed during Jesus's time. The art of feigning the defeat of death had been the work of sorcerers and wizards. If Jesus had freed himself from the pains of crucifixion, the religious leaders would have surely declared Jesus to be a sorcerer and would have begun to vehemently teach the laws against sorcery and wizardry, such as these:

> Leviticus 20:27 A man also or woman who hath a familiar spirit, or who is a wizard, shall surely be put to death: they shall stone them with stones; their blood shall be upon them.

> Leviticus 20:6 And the soul that turneth after such that as have familiar spirits, and after wizards, to go a whoring after them, I will even set my face against that soul, and will cut him off from among his people.

Leviticus 19:31 Regard not them that have familiar spirits, neither seek after wizards, to be defiled by them: I am the Lord Your God.

Exodus 22:18 Thou shalt not suffer a witch to live.

Jesus would have found himself greatly handicapped in trying to teach and to deliver the people he had been sent to save. His consistent request that they believe on him and believe that the Father had sent him would have fallen upon deaf ears. The people who were mourning and the ones who were railing would have soon joined together to attack Jesus, the accused sorcerer, with stones as required by the Law.

Jesus portrayed the perfected character of the Nazirite. He accepted the call to minister to the people and made serving them his primary duty. He lived his words before the people daily and continued to be vigilant to the will of God even to the cross. Indeed, he was to the people a teacher, a priest, and a prophet whose message and behavior were often in sharp contrast to those of the contemporary religious leadership. Jesus spent a tremendous amount of time with the common people, teaching, healing, and feeding them daily. People were able to see in him the level of compassion and understanding that had been absent for a long time. His daily teaching in the temple seems to indicate what was lacking in the temple. People were able to continually see, in the temple and at the cross, a spiritual teacher who focused his attention on others amid the constant negativity of religious leaders and amid excruciating pain.

Jesus took on the role of the Nazirite, who was the lowest on the hierarchy of priests and was perhaps not even truly recognized by the priesthood as attaining priestly status and sanctity. In Jesus, the lowly Nazirite had been raised above the higher-ranking priests in the eyes of the people because of his work and teaching among them.

Even though historians say that the scriptures give the Nazirite priest spiritual requirements as stringent as those of the high priest, there was no way the high priest or any of the other powerful and wealthy chieftains of the priesthood was going to recognize the lowly Nazirite priest as being equal to any of them.

# CHAPTER 8:
## PILATE AND HEROD

Why did Pilate, the Roman Governor, feel compelled to be in attendance at the Crucifixion with the priests and Pharisees? He was there to give an official annotation to the event by putting a label above Jesus that stated, in three languages, "Jesus of Nazareth, The King of the Jews." Pilate conformed the event to Caiaphas' words that "it is expedient for us that one man should die for the people, and that the whole nation perish not" (John 11:49). Pilate made Jesus officially that one man, and he wrote the title as a statement of fact. In contrast, the priests wanted the title written as an accusation: "He Said He Is King of the Jews."

> John 19:19, 21, 22 And Pilate wrote a title, and put it on the cross. And the writing was, JESUS OF NAZARETH, THE KING OF THE JEWS. Then said the chief priests of the Jews to Pilate, Write not, The King of the Jews, but, He said I am King of the Jews. Pilate answered, What I have written, I have written.

> Following the Roman custom, Pilate ordered a <u>sign posted above Jesus</u> on the cross stating "Jesus of Nazareth, The King of the Jews" to give public notice of the legal charge against him for his crucifixion. The chief priests protested that the public charge on the sign should read that Jesus claimed to be King of the Jews. Pilate refused to change the posted charge. This may have been to emphasize Rome's supremacy in crucifying a Jewish king; it is not unlikely, though, that Pilate was quite irritated by the fact, that the Jewish leaders had used him as a marionette and thus compelled him to sentence Jesus to death contrary to his own will (according to Mathew 27:19, even Pilate's wife asked him on Jesus' behalf).
> (http://en.wikipedia.org/wiki/Pontius_Pilate)

It seems that Pilate took a very personal interest in Jesus' crucifixion. His action to personally write the inscriptions may have been a result of deep contemplation about his questioning of Jesus and his wife's concerns. Is it possible that Pilate, in submitting to the will of the people and allowing the condemnation of Jesus, also condemned his wife to ongoing torture in her dreams? Was the washing of his hands sufficient to relieve her suffering in the night?

> Matthew 27:19 And when he was seated on the judgment seat, his wife sent unto him,

> saying, Have thou nothing to do with that
> righteous man; for I have suffered many
> things t   his day in a dream because of him.

The content of her dream is not revealed in scripture, but she was confident that whatever occurred in the dream was because of Jesus. It seems that Pilate's closed eyes might have been opened by the eyes of his wife. It is possible that Pilate was compelled to do more than just wash his hands. He made a definite statement before Jesus' accusers of the true identity of Jesus when he wrote the inscription declaring him the King of the Jews. Perhaps his wife was then able to sleep comfortably.

Pilate was also well aware that the soldiers responsible for carrying out the crucifixion were being heavily influenced by the devious chief priests and elders. If he wanted the inscription done right, he had better do it himself. There is, however, an irony in the priests' and Pharisees' reaction as Pilate gave orders for the title to be placed over Jesus. Caiaphas, the high priest, wanted Jesus to die for the nation and prevent a Roman takeover of the Jewish provinces but did not want to identify Jesus as anyone of authority or with any political clout. If Jesus was to die as a common lawbreaker, how did Caiaphas expect Rome to attach any significance to his death?

> John 11:48–50 If we let him thus alone, all
> men will believe on him; and the Romans
> shall come and take away our place and
> nation. And one of them, named Caiaphas,
> being the high priest that same year, and
> said unto them, Ye know nothing at all. Nor

consider that it is expedient for us that one man should die for the people, and that the whole nation perish not.

Pilate knew that Jesus must be given an appropriate identity that would get the attention of Rome, even though this awareness might have been a product of his wife's suffering.

The chief priest had arranged for the Crucifixion to take place during the time of the Passover, which made the Crucifixion a highly publicized event.

Cestius, desiring to inform Nero, who was inclined to condemn the nation, of the power of the city, requested the high priests to take a count, if possible, of the entire population. So these high priests did so upon the arrival of their feast which is called the Passover. On this day they slay their sacrifices from the ninth hour until the eleventh, with a company [*phatria*] of not less than ten belonging to every sacrifice—for it is not lawful for them to have the feast singly by themselves and many of us are twenty in a company. These priests found the number of the sacrifices was two hundred and fifty-six thousand five hundred; which, if we assume no more than ten feasted together, amounts to two million seven hundred thousand and two hundred persons; but this counted only those that were pure and holy

(Thematic Concordance to the Works of
Josephus, War 6.9.3 422–427, The Number
that Gathered in Jerusalem for the Passover,
http://www.josephus.org/Passover)

It was mandatory for all male Jews to go
up to Jerusalem for the feasts of Pentecost,
Tabernacles and Passover but Passover was
the most popular.
(GoodNews Online, http://www.ccr.org.uk/
archive/gn0503/g04.htm)

The festivities of the Passover brought huge numbers
of people from many provinces, by some estimates
close to a million people and by others roughly three
hundred thousand. Regardless of the debate over the
most accurate number, the event was a well-attended
and highly publicized one that was similar to the modern
trek to Mecca. Thus Pilate needed an explanation for the
execution that conformed to Roman law, and the title
above the condemned man would be what the people
would read and report as the official charge. Also, is it
possible that Pilate ignored the complaints of the chief
priests and elders because he had given them the chance to
clearly demonstrate their loyalty to Rome? He presented
to them Jesus and Barabbas. The release of Jesus would
have meant that the religious rulers were in favor of a
peaceful coexistence with Rome. The release of Barabbas
meant there was continued sympathy among the Jews
for the annoying and growing insurgency against Rome.
It is not conceivable that Rome was unaware of the
nature of Jesus' ministry; the talk in the streets did not

bypass the ears of the Roman soldiers on patrol. Pilate learned a lot about Jesus from his private conversation with the religious leaders who spoke slanderously about him. The Roman government surely spied on Jesus and his disciples as they investigated Barabbas. In fact, it can be safely assumed that they thoroughly investigated all possible movements of insurrection. On the other hand, the religious leaders knew of the possibility of a Roman invasion and probably wanted men like Barabbas among them who could be of great help in repelling the invasion:

> Matthew 27:20 But the chief priest and elders persuaded the multitude that they should ask for Barabbas, and destroy Jesus.

Without Pilate's inscription on the cross, the chief priesthood could verbally attach many accusations that required Jesus' death, but with the title they were limited to one. The title was also contrary to the religious leaders' effort to conform their actions to Jewish law. The inscription was one to spark legal debates in the Jewish community as to the reason Jesus was crucified. He was called a blasphemer, a sorcerer, and a false teacher, but none of those accusations were placed on the cross for legal and historical reference. It was the accusations of blasphemy that the religious leaders agreed were worthy of death when they questioned Jesus at the high priest's house:

> Matthew 26: 65–66 Then the high priest tore his clothes, saying, He hath spoken blasphemy! What further need have we of

witnesses? Behold, now, ye have heard his blasphemy. What think ye? They answered and said, He is guilty of death.

The religious leaders wanted the inscription to conform to their original Jewish charge. However, with Pilate's inscription they were faced with a Roman declaration rather than an actual charge. The priests were astute enough to anticipate that historians and some of the more sympathetic Jewish leaders would take a closer look at the events of the Crucifixion, and they knew that all matters needed to be supportive of their objective. If they could persuade Pilate to write the inscription as "He Said He is King of the Jews," then the inscription could imply sedition and blasphemy because the prophesized king was also considered divine.

Isaiah 9:6 For unto us a child is born, unto us a son is given, and the government shall be upon his shoulder; and his name shall be called Wonderful, Counselor, The Mighty God, The Everlasting Father, The Prince of Peace.

Jesus ministry was not confined to the poor commoners but was accepted by men of every status in the Jewish community. There were men who believed in Jesus, such as Nicodemus, a Sanhedrin; Joseph of Arimathea, a rich man and possibly a Sanhedrin; and Zacchaeus, a tax collector. The religious leaders knew that the debate over the Crucifixion, which probably had already begun, would rise to the forefront at some time in the near future. These leaders would have to address the following potential points of debate:

> The following are some of the <u>Mosaic Laws</u> that according to Christians were violated by the Sanhedrin in the trial of Christ: bribery (<u>Deuteronomy</u> 16:19; 27:25); conspiracy and the perversion of judgment and justice (<u>Exodus 23:1–2</u>; <u>Exodus 23:6–7</u>; <u>Leviticus 19:15</u>; Le 19:35); bearing false witness, in which matter the judges connived (Ex 20:16); letting a murderer (Barabbas) go, thereby bringing blood-guilt upon themselves and upon the land (Nu 35:31–34; De 19:11–13); <u>mob action</u>, or "following a crowd to do evil" (Ex 23:2, 3); in crying out for Jesus to be impaled, they were violating the law that prohibited following the statutes of other nations and that also prescribed no torture but that provided that a criminal be stoned or put to death before being hung on a stake (Le 18:3–5; De 21:22); they accepted as king one not of their own nation, but a pagan (Caesar), and rejected the King whom God had chosen (De 17:14, 15); and finally, they were guilty of murder (Ex 20:13).
> (Wikipedia, http://en.wikipedia.org/wiki/Sanhedrin_Trial_of_Jesus)

Pilate's inscription was not viewed as helpful to their cause and would spark controversy. He, of course, was not concerned about debates among the Jews, but among the Romans.

Herod is not mentioned as much as Pilate since he did not take part in the actual trial, but he was in Jerusalem with his men of war during the time of Jesus' interrogation, trial, and crucifixion.

> Luke 23:7 And as soon as he knew that he belonged unto Herod's jurisdiction, he sent him to Herod, who himself was also at Jerusalem at that time.
>
> Luke 23:11 And Herod, with his men of war, treated him with contempt …

It was very convenient that the two high authorities who could be instrumental in influencing a verdict of death were in the same city. Herod and Pilate, who were previously at odds with one another, had decided to form a friendship during the time of Jesus' trial and Crucifixion.

> Luke 23:12 And the same day Pilate and Herod were made friends together; for before they were at enmity between themselves.

Was there a third-party mediator who influenced the relationship between Pilate and Herod and who took advantage of the close proximity of the two with hope of achieving an ulterior motive? The men who were campaigning for Jesus to be crucified knew every facet of the religious and secular laws that had to be taken into consideration before his execution could be authorized. They were also obviously working on a tight schedule in order to have the crucifixion around the festival time of the Passover. With Herod and Pilate in the same city, there was no need to transport Jesus from city to city to be questioned.

Herod's army was in Jerusalem to assist with security during the festivities of the Passover. Because of Pilate and Herod's new friendship and their mutual concerns about Jesus' influence, their two armies became complicit in Jesus' death. Both men's soldiers mocked Jesus similarly, implying that the two leaders shared a high level of disdain for Jesus. Pilate and Herod's attitude may have been heavily influenced through the third-party mediation of the priesthood; they were the steady beat that kept everything moving toward crucifixion.

> Luke 23:10–11 And the chief priests and scribes stood and vehemently accused him. And Herod, with his men of war, treated him with contempt, and mocked him, and arrayed him in a gorgeous robe, and sent him again to Pilate.

Much more is written in scriptures about the soldiers under the control of Pilate and the high priest. The soldiers of the governor performed a curious set of actions prior to the Crucifixion:

> John 27:26–31 Then released he Barabbas unto them: and when he had scourged Jesus, he delivered him to be crucified. Then the

soldiers of the governor took Jesus into the
common hall, and gathered unto him the
whole band of soldiers. And they stripped
him, and put on him a scarlet robe. And
when they had plaited a crown of thorns,
they put it upon his head, and a reed in his
right hand; and they bowed the knee before
him, and mocked him, saying, Hail, King of
the Jews! And they spat upon him, and took
the reed, and smote him on the head. And
after they had mocked him, they took the
robe off from him, and put his own raiment
on him, and led him away to crucify him.

Why did the soldiers remove Jesus' clothing in the
common hall and replace it, only to remove it again at
the cross and gamble over it? (See quote from scripture
below.) If their intent at the cross was to have possession
of Jesus' clothing, the bargaining between the soldiers
could have been achieved in the common hall when the
clothes were first removed. They had already obtained
replacement clothing for Jesus in the form of a purple
robe, and they could have taken Jesus to the cross in
it and the crown of thorns, thus allowing the crowd to
join their mockery. Many who would be in the crowd
of hecklers during the procession were probably present
at the Judgment Hall when Pilate presented Jesus in the
purple robe. Herod and his men of war had also sent
Jesus to Pilate in a robe they had put on him in mockery.
It seems that the soldiers in the common hall were under
the control of the high priest and the chief priests and
elders. The fact that Jesus was clothed with robes by

Herod's men and Pilate's men probably shows that both Herod and Pilate wanted to ridicule Jesus' authority as a Nazirite priest and the prospect of him becoming King of the Jews. It was a display of their envy of his popularity, which was making him more influential than the high priest. The robe of the priest signified his sanctity before God. The religious leaders had definite plans for Jesus' clothing at the cross.

Was it customary for Roman soldiers to be scavengers at a crucifixion? The soldiers' actions were planned as part of Jesus' agony on the cross. The religious leaders ordered his clothes removed and destroyed; however, the soldiers at the cross failed the chief priests because they parted the clothes and left the robe or coat intact.

> John 19:23–24 Then the soldiers, when they had crucified Jesus, took his garments, and made four parts, to every soldier a part, and also his coat. Now the coat was without seam, woven from the top throughout. They said, therefore, among themselves, Let us not rend it, but cast lots for it, whom it shall be; that the scriptures might be fulfilled, which saith, they parted my raiment among them, and for my vesture they did cast lots. These things, therefore, the soldiers did.

It is difficult to find any reliable reference as to the exact nature of Jesus's clothing or that of the Nazirite priest, however, the soldiers' actions can be related to Exodus 28.

Exodus 28:4 And these are the garments which they shall make: a breastplate, and an ephod, and a robe, and an embroidered coat, a miter, and a girdle. And they shall make holy garments for Aaron, thy brother, and his sons, that he might minister unto me in the priest's office.

Exodus 28:31–32 And thou shalt make the robe of the ephod all of blue. And thou shalt make a hole in the top of it, in the midst thereof: it shall have a binding of woven work round about the hole of it, as it were the hole of a coat of mail, that it be not rent.

It is possible that Jesus was wearing a coat representing an equivalency to that of the high priest, which could not be rent. The soldiers carried the Messiah's coat back with them to their community of Gentiles. The chief priests and elders unknowingly offered strong symbolism of the new era of grace. The Law as symbolized by Jesus's clothes would come to an end, and Israel would be scattered by the Roman army. The gospel of Jesus Christ as symbolized by the coat would continue and be cherished by the Gentiles. The soldiers' action with Jesus' clothing shows the degree of humiliation and disrespect the religious leaders intended to heap upon him at the cross. The religious leaders didn't understand that their piousness before Pilate at the time when they desired to crucify an innocent man did not give Rome a favorable opinion of them.

Pilate's cooperation, though coerced, gave the religion leaders much encouragement in carrying out their plan to destroy Jesus. Herod's shallow admiration for Jesus sparked the initiation of the mockery. Two powerful men succumbed to the treachery of the religious leaders for their own political and financial well-being. Jesus was expendable and a good riddance for the sake of the peace of the nation. It was expected that after his death, the land would eventually return to normalcy. But there was nothing normal about the resurrection.

# CHAPTER 9:
# VICTORY

This book has covered the characters, interactions, and physical items that were part of the events surrounding the Crucifixion. There were no isolated events or characters. All were part of a diabolical effort to attack and destroy the priesthood of Jesus Christ. Each action was taken to bring disgrace or accusations against his priestly nature. Jesus' ultimate goal was to replace the institution of the priesthood by becoming man's only high priest for the redemption of sin.

> Hebrew 7:25–28 Wherefore he is able also to save them to the uttermost that come unto God by him, seeing he ever liveth to make intercession for them. For such an high priest was fitting for us, who is holy, harmless, undefiled, separate from sinners, and made higher than the heaven; Who needeth not daily, as those high priest, to offer up sacrifice, first for his own sins and then for the people's, for this he did once, when he offered up himself. For the law maketh men

> high priests who have infirmity, but the word
> of the oath, which was since the law, maketh
> the Son, who is consecrated for evermore.

The biblical passages of the dialogues and interactions of the time place much focus on the ongoing theological and philosophical debate between Jesus and the religious leaders who denied his deity. However, there should be greater focus on the character of Judas, not solely on his possible greed, ambition, and betrayal but on the true reason for his motivation. The scriptures show through Judas the underlying power that was influencing the call for Jesus 'death: Satan. Satan is not mentioned in the character portrayals of the chief priests, the elders, or the other members of the religious sects, nor in the portrayals of Pilate and Herod. They were shown with respect to their community status and religious clout. However, Judas' literary status, which began as an apostle, was relegated to that of a villain or traitor and was thus the avenue for the introduction of the influence of Satan. The introduction of Satan into the scheme of the Crucifixion means that the reader has to let his thoughts transcend the earthly activities and focus on the spiritual battle. The Crucifixion was a critical contest in the spiritual world war that has been raging since the beginning of time. A decisive victory was crucial.

The scriptures give an idea of the foothold Satan had made within the priesthood. The most obvious example is the conversion of the temple into a marketplace, which Jesus called "a den of thieves." And there was a display of power through wealth in the payment to Judas for his betrayal and the payment to the crowds and the bribery of the soldiers. There was the desire of the priests who offered sacrifices in the temple to conspire to secretly commit murder.

> Matthew 26:3–4 Then assembled together the chief priests, and the scribes, and the elders of the people, unto the palace of the high priest, who was called Caiaphas. And consulted that they might take Jesus by subtlety, and kill him.

And finally, the chief priests and elders, along with the high priest, considered Jesus to be like an infestation of their system of priesthood; he had to be eliminated lest they themselves be destroyed. The only system that would view the good Jesus had done for the people as a threat was the system of evil whose architect is Satan. Jesus was the panacea for the demonic infestation of the priesthood. The most insulting aspect to the priests, and the most piercing to the heart of the priesthood, was that they had no choice but to technically legitimize Jesus' priestly status because of the Vow of the Nazirite. Anyone could enter into the sacred vow and accept the responsibilities thereof and function as a priest. But Jesus proved to be a person with a priestly status who would not subject himself wholly to the control of the chief priests and elders. He also flaunted his interpretations of the Law in front of them in their very own temple. Satan knew that unless Jesus, the uncontrollable and the uninfluenced, were eliminated, all that he had established among the priesthood would soon come crumbling down and there would be no stone unturned.

Thus a plan was devised to viciously attack and destroy Jesus' priestly status. Everything that happened to him from the trial to the cross was meant to insult, degrade, or nullify his priesthood, for the redemption of mankind was dependent upon not miracles, but the authority of Jesus to atone for sins. The attacks included the scourging or lashes that were given to a Nazirite who fails to keep his consecration, the mockery of the robes, the temptation of the vinegar and gall, and the presence of the two thieves with Jesus on the cross.

The efforts Satan applied through the chief priests and elders failed, and they evoked Jesus' most miraculous performance of all, the Resurrection. The power to kill the most formidable opponent had come to naught. The money that paid for services and blood was useless, for there was not enough money to keep the whole country silent about the Resurrection. The religious leaders were powerless to explain the unexplainable without faith in Jesus Christ. They were condemned by the reality that Jesus was indeed the Messiah and the Son of God. In view of their hope of perpetuating their power, wealth, and overpowering influence on the people, they had orchestrated a tragedy.

The purpose of the priesthood's actions was primarily to prove that Jesus was not the Messiah and the Son of God, but their efforts to persuade the masses through intellectualism and threats were overshadowed by his teachings and miracles. The only recourse left for them to gain advantage over Jesus was to orchestrate his death. They did not realize that, as Judas, they were only pawns in the great spiritual battle between Satan and the Godhead. Satan needed the deeds of men to make Jesus an outcast in the sight of God, as Satan himself is. If Satan had been successful in tainting the spirituality of Jesus, he would have succeeded in corrupting God because Jesus is part of the Godhead. Physical death was insufficient because Satan knew it could not destroy Jesus Christ's perfect spirituality. There had to be a deed performed by Jesus in the body that was contrary to the laws of God; thus we have the events of the Crucifixion around the Vow of the Nazirite.

The Crucifixion was not Satan's first attempt to corrupt the spirituality of Christ. He pursued the same goal at the beginning of Jesus' earthly ministry, during the period referred to as the temptation of Jesus in the wilderness. The Crucifixion was a result of Satan's failure to destroy Jesus's sanctity when he began to minister. When Jesus told Satan to "Get thee behind me," it seems Satan retreated to his stronghold among the priesthood and began a coordinated and vicious attack upon Jesus, even to the cross. The phrase "If thou be" is noted in the scriptures at the beginning of Jesus' ministry and at the cross; the consistency of the phrase indentifies the underlying influence of Satan.

> Matthew 4: 3And when the tempter came to him, he said, If thou be the Son of God, command that these stones be made bread.

> Matthew 27: 39–40 And they that passed by reviled him, wagging their heads. And saying, If thou be the Son of God, come down from the cross.

> John 23:39 And one of the malefactors who were hanged railed at him, saying, If thou be the Christ, save thyself and us.

In the desert, at the very beginning of Jesus' ministry, Satan attempted to coerce Jesus into performing a miracle on demand in order to save himself. Likewise, during his ministry, the religious leaders and the people at the cross attempted to coerce Jesus into performing a miracle on demand to save himself by coming down from the cross. Jesus refrained from addressing the leading question about his identity and performing such a miracle. He knew that God would reveal the truth of his Sonship in due time to whomever has faith in him. The religious leaders soon found out the true identity of Jesus Christ as the Son of God after Christ's victory over death in the Resurrection.

Another parallel between Satan's actions at the beginning of Jesus' ministry and the actions of the priesthood during it and at the cross was the attempt to defile the sacrifice before God. During the temptation, Satan took Jesus to the pinnacle of the temple and tried to persuade him to jump, with knowledge that the angels would bear him up harmless.

> Matthew 4:5–6 Then the devil taketh him up into the holy city, and setteth him on a pinnacle of the temple. And saith unto him, If thou be the Son of God, cast thyself down; for it is written, He shall give his angels charge concerning thee, and in their hands

they shall bear thee up, lest at any time thou
dash thy foot against a stone.

Picture the scene. As the first rays of the
morning sun break across the Mount of
Olives, a priest standing on the Pinnacle of
the Temple sounds the trumpet. This is the
signal that the morning sacrifices are about to
begin. A total of fifteen animals are sacrificed
on the massive altar that stands before the
Temple. In the presence of thousands of
witnesses, the high priest slaughters these
animals with a ceremonial knife. The court
runs red with the blood of the slain animals.
A portion of the blood is poured into a cup
...
(http://www.angelfire.com, Jesus the Great
High Priest)

Whether or not God would have saved his Son after a
jump from the pinnacle is a subject of debate; however,
the act would have disrupted the holy sacrificial area of
the temple. The scriptures do not say at what time of day
Jesus was at the pinnacle of the temple. If it was during
the morning, his jump would certainly have disrupted
the morning sacrifice to God. And if by chance he had
landed with catastrophic injuries, he would have made
himself a blemished lamb and unworthy to be the sacrifice
to God for the sins of man. Satan's attempt to destroy
Jesus as the perfect sacrifice for sin was renewed at the
cross in the religious leaders. According to the scriptures,

they indicated verbally their amusement at the prospect of Jesus being unworthy before God.

> Matthew 27:42 - He trusted in God; let him deliver him now, if he will have him; for he said, I am the Son of God.

The phase "if he will have him" is a sure indicator that the religious leaders knew that their actions would spoil the sacrifice. But the Resurrection was proof that God had accepted Jesus as a worthy sacrifice for the sins of man and that the plan of salvation was alive and well.

Also, Satan offered Jesus a membership in his fraternity of priests and rulers by offering him the grand opportunity to be a ruler over kingdoms and people.

> Matthew 4:8–9 Again, the devil taketh him up an exceedingly high mountain, and showeth him all the kingdom of the world, and the glory of them. And saith unto him, All these things will I give thee, if thou wilt fall down and worship me.

Notice that prior to the mountain trip, Satan had tempted Jesus to jump from the pinnacle of the temple. It should seem that a jump from the mountain would have been a better challenge for the Son of God over whom the angels keep charge. The mountain trip seems to clarify that the temptation on the pinnacle of the temple was for the corruption of the sacrifice. On the mountain Satan flaunted his accomplishments among the wealthy and powerful Jewish leaders. These accomplishments were highlighted during Jesus' ministry through the influence the religious leaders had over rulers such as Pilate and Herod, over the population, and even over one of Jesus' disciples. The wealth could be seen in the commercial transformation of the temple during the holy time of the Passover and in the distribution of money for religious and political schemes such as the betrayal by Judas. Jesus rejected Satan's offer, for he knew that earthly power and wealth were only temporary. After his victory over death in the Resurrection, Jesus proclaimed the acceptance of the power and wealth afforded him by his oneness with God.

> Matthew 28:18 - And Jesus came and spoke to them, saying, All power is given unto me in heaven and in earth.

The scriptures paint a surreal picture of the actions of those involved in Jesus' death. It seems unbelievable that there was such an attack against an innocent man: the religious leaders' constant testing of his teachings and their threats of bodily harm; the mob scene with Judas in the Garden of Gethsemanes; the mockery by the soldiers of Herod and Pilate; the antics of the crowd at the cross; and the gambling by the soldiers at the cross. And then there is the foolish declaration from the crowd at the Judgment Hall, who said that Jesus' blood would be on their hands and those of their children.

> Matthew 27:25 - Then answered all the people, and said, His blood be on us, and on our children.

If not for the belief in the truth of the scriptures, Jesus' experiences in the Crucifixion events might seem a very imaginative drama. But the actions of those who were against Jesus were indicative of a diabolical inner rage—the seething evil and vindictive spirit of Satan. It is the same evil spirit that rose up against Jesus at his birth when Herod the Great, father of Herod Antipas of Jesus' time, ordered the slaughter of all children under the age of two years.

> Matthew 2:16 Then Herod, when he saw that he was mocked of the wise men, was exceedingly angry, and sent forth, and slew all children that were in Bethlehem, and in all its borders, from two years old and under, according to the time which he had diligently inquired of the wise men.

God rescued the child Jesus, and the rage festered and reached a peak again as a result of Jesus' ministry. The reality and power of the Resurrection diminished the evil rage for a moment. However, it will reach a peak again at Christ's return for the great war of Armageddon, when Jesus will once again triumph over Satan—for the final time.

> It is the great final battle between the King of Kings and the trilogy of the Antichrist of Rev.16:13: The dragon, the beast, and the false prophet.

But the great battle of Armageddon is never described, only the results, because **this Great Battle had already been won by the Lamb at Calvary ...** and it will be completely effective in your life and mine the day we die ... Armageddon is the symbol of the total, complete, and final victory of Jesus in his Church against Satan and his followers, with their total and complete defeat, which is the core of the whole book of Revelation. (Armageddon or Har-megedon, http://www.religion-cults.com/antichrist/armaggedon.htm)

The primary purpose of highlighting the association of the Vow of the Nazirite to the Crucifixion is to emphasize that the Crucifixion must be studied from a view from above and a view from below. Heaven and hell saw redemption for mankind through the sacrificial blood of Jesus Christ, who would die as the unblemished Lamb. Heaven wanted it to be so; hell did not. Men were the prize pawns in the battle for it to be, or not to be. Christ's victory over death was man's victory and man's hope for life after death through the one-time sacrifice by Jesus Christ on Calvary.

# About the Author

Elmer M. Haygood was born in Greensboro, North Carolina. He is a graduate of Hardin-Simmons University in Abilene, Texas, and was employed for twelve years with the Greensboro Police Department. He has served in the Youth and Sunday School Departments of the Church of God in Christ in the Greater North Carolina Jurisdiction and the Jurisdiction of Southwestern Florida. He has been employed as a Human Services Supervisor for the Hillsborough County Health and Social Services Department in Tampa, Florida, for the past twenty-one years.

# References

The Scofield Study Bible, 1976 editon, authorized King James Version, Oxford Press, Inc.
Jewish Encyclopedia.com
Catholic Encyclopedia.com

(D'Varim, http://dvarim11.blogspot.com
Agape Bible Study.com

Biblog.com

Conservapedia.com

New Advent.org

Encyclopedia Biblica.com

Gospel-mysteries.net

Schwertley, Brian M. - The Heart of the Gospel: Gethsemane to the Burial of Christ, Chapter 22, the Reaction to the Death of Christ and the Accompanying Phenomenon" (The Covenant Reformation Press, 2007

*Elmer M. Haygood*

Xenos Christian Fellowship.com

Thematic Concordance to the Works of Josephus, War 6.9.3 422–427, The Number that Gathered in Jerusalem for the Passover

GoodNews Online

Angelfire.com
Religion-cults.com

Wikipedia.com